BEYOND PIECEMEAL IMPROVEMENTS

HOW TO TRANSFORM YOUR SCHOOL USING DEMING'S QUALITY PRINCIPLES

RON WARWI

EDITED BY KENNETH FREESTON

NATIONAL EDUCATIONAL SERVICE
BLOOMINGTON, INDIANA   1995

Copyright © 1995 by National Educational Service
1252 Loesch Road
P.O. Box 8
Bloomington, IN 47402
Phone: 800-733-6786 or 812-336-7700
FAX: 812-336-7790

Cover design by Bill Dillon

Printed in the United States of America

Printed on recycled paper

ISBN 1-879639-41-6

TABLE OF CONTENTS

TABLE OF CONTENTS (CONTINUED)

DEDICATION

This book is dedicated to my grandchildren, Taylor, Preston, and Michael. Also, to the grandchildren yet to come in our family and in yours. When I look into their eyes, I realize the urgency for improvement throughout our educational system so they may benefit from our efforts. All that we do today shapes tomorrow's education of our children and grandchildren. It is my sincere wish that every child is valued and gains from our educational system. For children are the future!

ACKNOWLEDGMENTS

As I reflect on the many people who influenced and formed my thoughts through the years for this task, I hope they are pleased with the final product. Each of us is encouraged by significant people in our lifetime. My parents have always supported me. Their love is present at all times. Sister Regina, my seventh- and eighth-grade teacher, made my mother promise to send me to parochial high school so I would stay on the right road. The priests at Weber High School watched over me and caused me to study harder than at any time in my educational career.

Dr. I. James Young is a friend who encouraged me academically and challenged my thinking with respect to quality education. Many hours were given to debate and discussion on the value of educational strategies and various philosophies. When we needed to disagree, we always valued the other's ideas. Dr. William Hitzmen was the person who gave me the opportunity to implement many of the ideas shared in this book. I am sorry he is not here to share in the joy of this work. He was a valued friend.

Without Connie, my wife and greatest friend, this project would not exist. She is the heart and soul of my efforts. Her constant encouragement, intellectual support, academic skills, and unending belief in me are beyond my understanding. She is the joy of my life.

I am grateful to Alan Blankstein for supporting this project. We share a common commitment to Dr. Deming's philosophy and the passion to share it with others. Nancy Shin and Julia Hunt have moved the work along in the many steps necessary to bring it to finality. Their efforts are appreciated and commended.

Most directly, Roy Irving with assistance from Larry Haise helped this work come alive. Their teaching experience and editing skills helped clarify and sharpen ideas and integrate a holistic message. Their assistance was invaluable. Without it, this book would not exist! I am also thankful to Kenneth Freeston for sharing ideas that contributed to the final organizational structure.

The conversations and analysis of ideas with Earl Conway were wonderful. His insight helped me to clarify and express key points more accurately with respect to this philosophy. His support for this work is greatly appreciated.

Of course, I would be remiss if I did not acknowledge Dr. Deming for transforming me and challenging me to improve the educational system. The joy of learning and improving the educational system for our children's gain is a worthwhile lifelong challenge.

I am also thankful to many others who have helped me along the way. Some who have shared their time and feedback on this project are Elizabeth McDonald, Sal Vallina, Bruce Marchiafava, Glenn Heck, Richard Soderberg, William Attea, and Al Ramirez. A special thanks to Allyson Dworkin for her computer skills and devotion to quality. I hope this work is helpful to others throughout our journeys.

ABOUT THE AUTHOR

Dr. Warwick has been a teacher, administrator, and consultant in education for over thirty years. He taught mathematics in the Chicago Public Schools and in Indiana University's Upward Bound Program. He was an assistant professor at Toledo University and a full professor in the Educational Leadership Department at National-Louis University. His administrative experience includes responsibilities as principal of a middle school, associate superintendent of curriculum and instruction in an Illinois school district, and chair of the Educational Leadership Department at National-Louis University for eighteen years. In addition to his roles as teacher and administrator, he consults with many school systems, state departments, and other educational organizations. Dr. Warwick has published over twenty articles in educational journals and has been involved in a number of research and grant-approved programs. He has also conducted leadership management seminars for Greater Europe Mission throughout Europe and at the Global Mission Center in Seoul, South Korea.

Dr. Warwick earned a B.S. in Mathematics and a Master's in Education from Loyola University, Chicago, Illinois. He earned an Ed.D. in Administration and Curriculum from Indiana University, Bloomington, Indiana. He has also pursued postdoctoral study in the Kettering-Sloan: I.D.E.A. School Change Process, in Situational Leadership Management Theory, and in Dr. Deming's Philosophy of Quality Management.

He and his wife Connie live in Buffalo Grove, Illinois, where they have raised their family. Daughter Kelly and son Thomas are married and have children. Youngest son Jeffrey is employed and on his own. Ron and

Connie are blessed in having all of their children nearby and especially enjoy the opportunity to share in the lives of their grandchildren.

FOREWORD

by Earl C. Conway
Director–Corporate Quality Worldwide (Retired)
The Procter & Gamble Company

At long last, the leaders of our educational system have been given the knowledge they need to make the transformation to continual improvement and superior results.

Beyond Piecemeal Improvements had to be written, and it could have been done only by an experienced and talented educator with an understanding of the teachings of Dr. W. Edwards Deming. Ron Warwick has done it for us.

Dr. Deming frequently commented that "there is no substitute for knowledge." It is not the recitation of facts, examples to be modeled, or the extensive experience of well-meaning administrators or teachers. Rather, more than anything else, lasting knowledge requires an understanding of fundamental theory. In perhaps his most profound statement intended to help us understand, Dr. Deming asserted that "experience and example mean little or nothing without theory." And then he proceeded to prove it again and again. It requires an understanding of the theory of systems, of variation, of analysis of data for predictive purposes, and of psychology to appreciate the importance of differences in people.

Ron Warwick has studied the teachings of Dr. Deming and applied them to the classrooms of our school systems. Accepting the Deming philosophy was very comfortable from the beginning for Ron because it seemed so compatible with his own efforts over more than thirty years as an educator. Still, writing the book was a major undertaking, largely because it breaks new ground in a highly complex and challenging field. Much has been written about quality, and some educators have already attempted to apply the subject to our schools. But almost all efforts have proved ineffective because little or no attention was paid to the theories, which are essential to their having any lasting value.

"Joy in learning" is what Dr. Deming offered us as an educator himself. He then gave us the philosophy and the theories to achieve it. More than any other author, Ron Warwick has effectively transferred this thinking to the one system that determines our future. It is now up to the leaders in our educational system to take the knowledge offered in *Beyond Piecemeal Improvements* and begin the long-term task of transformation.

PREFACE

by Al Ramirez, Ed.D.
Director, Iowa Department of Education
Des Moines, Iowa

Dr. W. Edwards Deming taught us that "transformation requires profound knowledge" and that "once the individual understands the system of profound knowledge, he will apply its principles in every kind of relationship with other people. He will have a basis for judgment of his own decisions and for the transformation of the organizations he belongs to." These words become more significant to American educators with each passing day, as we struggle to find solutions to the vexing challenges facing our schools.

Dr. Deming's philosophy has meaning for all involved in education: for teachers who manage classrooms, students who manage their own learning, school administrators in their operating approaches, and school boards in establishing their philosophies of governance. All of us who have a role in helping students achieve higher levels of learning must understand Dr. Deming's message. All of us working to transform our schools from nineteenth-century "smokestack" operations to organizations that help prepare students for success in the twenty-first century must apply new solutions to our efforts. A dozen years of failed school-reform initiatives are evidence enough that bandwagons and magic bullets will never help us reach our aim.

Just as Dr. Deming helped war-ravaged Japan become an economic giant, and the American auto industry effect one of the greatest turn-arounds in history, he can help American educators and students who are ready for our new economy and the demands of civic life in our modern democracy. Through the study of his work, we can all gain insight into the action steps needed to rebuild our schools.

Ron Warwick has faithfully captured the essential teachings of Dr. Deming and applied them to the educational system without losing anything in the translation. No other author has accomplished such a thorough analysis of our educational system using the Deming philosophy. *Beyond Piecemeal Improvements* will soon be a basic text for all educational leadership programs and a well-worn reference for all who strive to achieve the ideals of our educational system.

INTRODUCTION

For the past thirty years, I have invested my life in teaching. Along the way, I have been blessed with many opportunities to work with people who care deeply about others, about the learning process, and about quality of life. I have been intrigued and challenged by new approaches these people have taken—strategies that stress each student's uniqueness and the need to help all learners feel valued. Educational systems are often at cross-purposes with these goals, however, and at times I have felt discouraged about the prospects for institutional change. Fortunately, certain events have occurred to sustain my commitment.

One such event took place a number of years ago. As I was preparing to travel to teach leadership seminars in Europe, my colleague Charles Thomas gave me a copy of Mary Walton's book, *The Deming Management Method*. In reading it, I identified with everything being said and found myself cheering inwardly. It was exciting to realize that someone was writing about what I believed and had implemented in education for many years. In its discussion of management principles put forth by Dr. W. Edwards Deming, the book spoke to me in a compelling way. I finished reading it while on the trip and could hardly wait until I returned home to learn more.

On October 4, 1991, I attended my first Deming four-day seminar. This defining experience thoroughly affirmed my beliefs and fueled, again, my commitment to improve our educational system. Afterward, I studied as many of Deming's writings as I could find. I continued to attend his seminars and began to apply his ideas in my profession.

The following year, I felt honored to be invited to speak at Dr. Deming's education conference. After that, I began to correspond with him, expressing some of my thoughts about education. Later, I shared moments with him in person, which I will cherish the rest of my life. In my mind, I can still hear his voice encouraging me to clarify educational aims and improve the system continually using basic statistical tools. "Work on the system!" he would say with zest. "Evaluate the system, not the people in it!"

I believe the Deming philosophy of management will transform education in the United States, but the challenge is great. It is intellectually demanding and requires a long-term commitment. Yet it gives me tremendous joy to know that what Dr. Deming is asking of us is the right thing to do, that his is the right way to do it, and that the right time is now. In this book, I have attempted to apply Deming's precepts to the educational system as a whole and specifically to the heart of teaching: the instructional process. I trust that I have been faithful to Dr. Deming's ideas. I hope the book is helpful to fellow educators.

As you consider and discuss the ideas presented in this book with others, you will be challenged by many people. Some will raise individual issues as a way of saying the Deming philosophy will not work in education. You may be skeptical yourself at times. Let me encourage you, however, not to be deterred by objections such as these:

- What do you mean, not grade students? Everyone needs external reward systems to be motivated.

- There have to be consequences for poor performance or work missed.

- Grades cannot be removed!

- If you do not hold students accountable, they will take advantage of the situation and do nothing.

- Competition increases strength and determination. It sharpens skills. It helps one survive.

I believe that those who hold unswervingly to these positions either have not studied Dr. Deming's philosophy or have studied and misunderstood it. In any case, I encourage readers to consider with an open mind the ideas presented in this book. When concerns such as those just stated are raised, I often think and respond in terms from the world of business and organizations:

- Yes, people can be recognized for excellent work and contributions to the system—as long as the rewards are appropriate and given in the proper way.

- Yes, some people may have to be "let go" after much effort to direct them or help them improve. But other options are usually available. Finding alternative places for them in the work structure is one. Discussing work-related concerns with them in ways that help them recognize their capabilities is another. A satisfactory solution to unmet expectations may involve helping some people, in the end, find other employment. Whatever happens, however, people must always be respected and valued.

- Traditional performance evaluations in the business world usually have no more meaning than the letter grades given in schools. In some schools, grades are not used. But, even so, grades are not central to a discussion of this nature. The real issue is accurate evidence of people's learning, achievement, and joy in learning, whether they are adults at work or students in school. In the context of education, solid evidence of achievement is what students need to provide, and the system must give them opportunities to do so.

- Holding people accountable in the work world has little to do with improving the quality of a service or product. If a supervisor fights for the right to hold individuals accountable within an organization, power and control is often the real agenda. All that most workers want is the opportunity to contribute and be recognized. Education and training are necessary to "make it all work" in a business or organization. Intrinsic motivation must be enhanced and pride in workmanship nurtured. In most people, these inner resources have diminished over the years. It takes time for them to develop again. But if people—children or adult learners—understand the system in which they are working and its objectives, and if the system is designed to maximize their chances of success, then the arrangement will work to everyone's benefit.

- Competition in schools and places of work is detrimental to the spirit for almost everyone but the top "winners." Most people have a sense of loss when all is said and done. There is a better way!

A PERSONAL NOTE

In November of 1991, I received a special letter from Dr. Deming. His note to me was in response to a letter I had written to him saying how much his seminar had inspired me. In my letter to him, I had shared some of my thoughts about education in this country with respect to his ideas, especially his 14 points of management. Dr. Deming sent me some of his notes on topics related to education. These were eventually presented in his latest book, *The New Economics for Industry, Government, and Education* (1993). This is his letter to me . . .

W. EDWARDS DEMING, PH.D.
CONSULTANT IN STATISTICAL STUDIES

WASHINGTON 20016
4924 BUTTERWORTH PLACE

TEL. (202) 363-8552
FAX (202) 363.3501

7 November 1991

Dear Dr. Warwick,

It pleases me to be a partner with you in education. Here are some pages that I prepared on the subject. They are in rough form as you will observe. I remain with best greetings

Sincerely yours,

W. Edwards Deming

To Dr. Ron Warwick
940 Port Clinton Court W.
Buffalo Grove, Illinois
60089

After receiving this communication, I continued to attend Deming seminars and absorb his philosophy through videotapes and written materials. I also updated him on my efforts to implement his ideas in education. As I prepare materials for my own seminars, I try diligently to represent Dr. Deming's thoughts accurately and consistently. This book represents an integration and application of what I have learned since that first four-day Deming seminar in 1991. Adopting the Deming philosophy has had a profound impact on my life. It has changed how I think and respond to people. It has altered my expectations and vision for the future. I am grateful to Dr. Deming for this and hope I represent him well.

I welcome your feedback about any thoughts or actions you think would improve the communication of the ideas presented.

Ronald P. Warwick
National Educational Service
1610 W. Third Street
P.O. Box 8
Bloomington, IN 47402
Phone: (812) 336-7700
Fax: 812-336-7790

part

1

The Road We Are Traveling

Our nation is at risk. Our once unchallenged preeminence in . . . science and technological innovation is being overtaken by competitors throughout the world. . . . The educational foundations of our society are presently being eroded by a rising tide of mediocrity that threatens our very future as a Nation and a people.

Report of the National Commission on
Excellence in Education, 1983

CHAPTER 1

EDUCATION AT A CROSSROADS
THE CRISIS IN OUR SCHOOLS

Most Americans do not need national studies to tell them that something is still wrong with our schools. As the 20th century comes to a close, the laments of reformers of previous decades—Johnny can't read, Maria can't write, and Jamal can't compute—are being amplified by additional and more serious concerns. In too many instances, Nick doesn't know the difference between right and wrong and doesn't care to, and neither does Tanya. Gender sensitivity and multicultural awareness training for school personnel may or may not have made Keito or Kimberly appreciate the differences in people. And André and Anya and all their classmates may be limited in intellectual development by political polarization in society, for, whether they are in a back-to-basics school environment or a discovery-oriented approach to learning, they are subject to the biases of adults who have designed the program.

Teachers point to the hypnotic power and moral corrosiveness of television, movies, video games, and popular magazines and books, as well as to deterioration of support at home, as detrimental influences that are hard to counteract in the classroom. If nothing else, television, movies, and rental video phenomena tend to make people passive. Those who spend a lot of their time watching rather than doing can get the idea that all of life, including school, should be highly entertaining. The joys of personal discovery and accomplishment, so vivid in early childhood, can easily be lost. Many parents are indifferent to such problems. Others, while acutely concerned, do not always know what to do. Meanwhile, employers and other end-users of the educational product long for "the good old days" when young people's attitudes toward work, personal responsibility, and service to others were markedly different.

This is our dilemma, and it seems to be worsening. Resolving the crisis, I feel, calls for an educational transformation, from the foundation up. Solutions to these problems require more than piecemeal or half-hearted reforms. A new way of thinking and determining priorities is needed. Focusing as they do on meaningful knowledge and the quest for excellence, the ideas of W. Edwards Deming are the best conceptual resources we have. That is why I have written this book. Before applying Deming principles to the learning process, however, I want to provide what I feel is convincing information about the nature of the schooling crisis.

UNSETTLING SCORES

The slowly simmering crisis in education boiled over into the national consciousness in 1983 with the release of the report by the National Commission on Excellence in Education. Charged by T. H. Bell, President Reagan's secretary of education, to examine the quality of education in the United States, the commission titled its report *A Nation at Risk*, and used strong language to describe the effects of "the rising tide of mediocrity" that was overtaking U.S. education:

> *Our Nation is at risk. . . . Our once unchallenged preeminence in commerce, industry, science, and technological innovation is being overtaken by competitors throughout the world. . . . We report to the American people that while we take justifiable pride in what our schools and colleges have historically accomplished and contributed to the United States and the well-being of its people, the educational foundations of our society are presently being eroded by a rising tide of mediocrity that threatens our very future as a Nation and a people.* (Gardner, 1983)

Ten years later, the Department of Education issued a second report, *The Condition of Education 1994*, which cited certain areas of progress and other areas of stagnation—or even regression—since 1983. While the report noted some significant gains in reading, writing, mathematics, and science, it also highlighted some disturbing deficiencies (Riley, 1994).

READING

Initial progress in raising reading scores appeared to have leveled out or even fallen for 9-, 13-, and 17-year-olds between 1971 and 1972. While black and Hispanic students appeared to be raising their scores, and the gap between their performance and that of their white peers narrowed somewhat, the reading proficiency of all 9-year-olds actually declined between 1980 and 1992. Scores for 17-year-olds failed to increase at all after 1984.

WRITING

Although the scores for writing proficiency of fourth- and eighth-grade students improved between 1984 and 1992, those of the eleventh graders remained unchanged, and boys continued to earn lower scores than girls. While most groups began to show substantial improvement starting in 1990, 1992 scores showed that only slightly over one-third of the eleventh graders could write responses that were not only "focused" and "clear" but also "more complete" (level 300). A mere 2 percent of these students scored at level 350, where they demonstrated an ability to generate "effective, coherent responses." The scores of eleventh graders at the 95th percentile of their age group in 1992 were actually lower than they had been in 1990, and those of the fourth graders at this percentile showed no improvement.

MATHEMATICS

After nine years of little progress, math scores of 9-year-olds began to improve after 1982, but, even after steady improvement, the scores in 1992 revealed an unsettling range of proficiency between the highest- and lowest-performing students—a 100-point spread between the 5th and 95th percentile. The 17-year-olds improved somewhat at the lower and average levels, but those scoring at or above level 350—the highest level—remained unchanged at 7 percent.

SCIENCE

Science achievement has improved since 1982, the year before *A Nation at Risk* was published, but the report of 1993 shows some difficiencies that may not bode well for the future. Black and Hispanic students continue to achieve at a level well below that of whites, although the gap is decreasing slightly for 13-year-olds. Even among white 9-year-olds, the lowest achievers (5th percentile) were a full 120 points behind the highest achievers in the 95th percentile.

THE RISK REMAINS

Observers who focus on areas where progress has been made conclude that the American school system is working better today than at in any time in history. They point to findings in *The Condition of Education 1994* that the number of students in all groups—white, black, and Hispanic—who complete high school has been rising steadily and that the number of dropouts has not increased since 1992.

Although such figures are reassuring, they cannot mask others that reveal the ongoing deterioration of U.S. education compared to that in other countries. Although our dropout rate is not increasing, it remained steady between 1990 and 1993. While only 11 percent of whites dropped out of school, the figure was 17 percent for blacks and a shocking 36 percent for Hispanics, and these figures are increasing. *The Condition of Education 1994* noted that many students leave school before completing tenth grade. Of the high school class of 1992, for example, nearly 7 percent had dropped out of school by the spring of their sophomore year. Today, the average dropout rate for all students in the United States is at least 14 percent, compared to a 9 percent rate in Germany and 6 percent in Japan.

Students in these and many other countries continue to best our students in various international comparisons of achievement. Further, there is increasing evidence that average scores on many of our achievement tests have been inflated over the years to provide a false sense of improved academic growth.

The national studies of the U.S. Department of Education did not provide specific statistics on large urban school districts or inner-city school systems, where the atmosphere is grim and the rise in dropout rates alarming. In 1994, a report of the Council of Great City Schools stated that 78 percent of the nation's 51 largest urban school districts reported an increase in the dropout rate for black students even as overall rates were falling. These districts serve 5.8 million children, or 13.6 percent of school-age youngsters nationwide, but the prospects for these schools are dim. "Schools based in crime-ridden and drug-driven neighborhoods inevitably have problems with discipline," says a 1992 article in *The Economist.* "Some have to install metal detectors to keep guns and knives out of the classroom. Dropout rates of 50 percent are not uncommon." In 1994, the *Metropolitan Life Survey of the American Teacher* indicated that

- 23 percent of parents and 19 percent of students rated their school's quality only fair or poor

- 36 percent of junior high students and 34 percent of high school students said their school does only a fair or poor job of providing a safe environment for learning

- 17 percent of parents and 24 percent of students believe that violence in their school had increased in the past year.

Additional subtle but generally negative forces are contributing to the decline in our students' achievement. Parental and community pressure is demanding changes such as "zero tolerance" expulsion policies in the interest of school safety. In February 1994, for example, Michigan's schools began to expel first through fifth graders caught with weapons. Junior and senior high school students would be out for a year. Students in South Florida's Broward County can now be expelled simply for threatening violence (*USA Today*).

While Chicago schools may have developed more problems more quickly than those of many other urban systems, they offer an instructive example of the direction that many of our schools are headed. According to *Report of Chicago Public Schools Achievement Trends: October 26, 1994,* student proficency in reading, writing, and mathematics gives no cause for satisfaction. In May 1994, students in grades three through eight were tested in reading and mathematics with the *Iowa Test of Basic Skills.* High school students were tested with the *Tests of Achievement and Proficiency* in April of that year. Results were compared with those achieved over the previous four years, with the following findings:

- Only about one-fourth of all students scored at or above the national norms in reading.

- Slightly more than a quarter of students in grades three through eight scored above the national norm in mathematics, but only about one-fifth of the high school students attained this level.

- The percentage of eleventh graders scoring at or above national norm levels in reading was slightly lower in 1994 than in 1990. The percentage at or above the national norm in mathematics was virtually unchanged at slightly over 23 percent.

- The percentage of ninth graders scoring at or above national norm levels in reading had dropped considerably in five years, from 30.8 percent in 1990 to 19.8 percent in 1994.

- At every grade level, the percentage of students who scored at or above the national norm in mathematics declined between 1993 and 1994.

A second report prepared for the Chicago Board of Education presents equally disturbing evidence of lack of progress on turning around an unacceptedly high dropout rate (Johnson, 1994). Nearly half the students in the system quit before graduating. In 1994, the four-year dropout rate was 42.6 percent—about the same as the 42.5 percent rate of 1982. In some places in the country, the dropout rate of blacks and Hispanics has been falling and closing the gap with that of whites, but in Chicago the dropout rate for whites has been equal to that of the other ethnic groups or actually rising. For all twelve years included in the report, the dropout rate for boys exceeded that for girls, and generally students with lower eighth-grade reading scores had consistently higher dropout rates in high school.

EDUCATION FOR WINNERS

It is clear that we cannot continue to conduct our national education in a business-as-usual mode. William DeLauder, writing for the

Education Commission of the States, has depicted the challenge ahead of us:

> *Our education system must do a much better job of educating students for a revitalized democracy and a world economy. Accomplishing this goal requires the support of literally everyone—parents, students, educators, policy makers, business people and public as a whole. To gain this necessary support, we must communicate to all citizens why we need a revamped education system and what such a system should be like.* (DeLauder, 1992)

The aim of this book is to share ideas that will enable those concerned with our schools to unite in forming an educational system that adds value to each person and is always improving. Such a system encourages careful examination of each learning process and asks "by what method" we can best achieve our objectives. In elaborating on the philosophy involved, I will reexamine, among other ideas, the commonly held belief that competition in the classroom improves learning. We need an educational system in which everyone wins—and no one loses!

The Deming philosophy, which is the key to meaningful change, requires self-transformation and acceptance of the truth that there is no quick fix. So this study is not for the fainthearted but for leaders, parents, and students who believe we must change old ways of thinking and take rigorous new approaches to the challenges before us.

The chapters that follow provide a framework for change. Chapter 2 tells how education in America came to be at a crossroads of crisis and opportunity. Chapter 3 highlights the key role that the concepts of a system and quality play in meaningful change. Chapter 4 shows how system optimization can make teaching and learning a productive pleasure. Chapter 5 explores Deming's notion of variation in a system. Chapter 6 explains his theory of knowledge as an agent of prediction. Chapter 7 delves into motivational psychology. Chapter 8 examines the Deming improvement cycle: Plan–Do–Study–Act. Chapter 9 provides additional applications of transformational theory. Chapter 10 refines system-improvement principles. Chapter 11 gives implications for leadership. The epilogue concludes our discussion with some personal thoughts.

I hope you enjoy our journey together.

REFERENCES

Council of the Great City Schools (1994). *New York Times*, September 28, pB, 8 (N), pB, 8(L), column 3.

DeLauder, W. (1992). *Renewing public dialogue: 1992 education agenda.* Denver, CO: Education Commission of the States, p. 1.

The Economist (1992). November 21, p. 8.

Gardner, D.P., et al. (1983). *A nation at risk.* Washington, DC: The National Commission on Education, p. 5.

Johnson, A.K. (1994). *High school dropouts: 1982-1994.* Chicago Public Schools, Department of Research, Evaluation and Planning, December 19.

Report of Chicago Public Schools achievement trends: October 26, 1994 (1994). Chicago: Chicago Public Schools, Department of Research, Evaluation and Planning.

Riley, R.W. (1994). *The condition of education 1994.* Washington, DC: U.S. Department of Education, National Center for Education Statistics.

USA Today (1994). February 1, Section D, pp. 1-2.

The American people know instinctively that education is the future. . . . Our economic prosperity, and our nation's civic life have never been more linked to education than they are today as we enter the Information Age of the 21st century.

U.S. Secretary of Education Richard Riley

CHAPTER 2

THE REARVIEW MIRROR
HISTORICAL PERSPECTIVE

The trouble we are in has its roots in the late 19th century, when a mechanistic assembly-line theory of educational management came into vogue. Frederick Taylor, an engineering industrialist and efficiency expert, shaped the thinking of many educators of his day, and curricular designs reflecting this philosophy extend throughout the 20th century.

My school experience illustrates that Taylor's influence is persisting. Because I enjoyed mathematics and science as a young person coming through high school in the 1950s, I studied these subject areas during all four years. In my senior year, I took courses in physics and trigonometry. In the framework of the time, there was nothing unusual about this combination of classes or about studying these subjects independently. When I began a physics course in college, however, I saw trigonometry being integrated with science concepts from the beginning. I will never forget my reaction as I sat in class during the first week, reflecting on my high school classes and inwardly asking why my previous teachers had not undertaken this blend of disciplines. It upset me to think that I had not been given the opportunity to think and learn in this manner. It made such sense.

The high school curriculum of my day forced students to think compartmentally. The college curriculum encouraged integrated thought. In each situation, the system determined thinking processes, and students had little choice. They either suffered or gained from the system in which they were immersed. Ask yourself which design benefits the student more, not only in school but throughout life.

Another example of forced integration was created for me during the last year of my undergraduate studies. The university I attended required a two-day written comprehensive examination in the major concentration—in my case, mathematics. In six months of preparation for this exam, I tied together more mathematical concepts and came to understand more interrelationships between different areas of study than at any previous time in college. The feeling of satisfaction in this was uplifting. The knowledge I acquired was powerful. The lesson I learned was that unless one is forced to combine ideas through experience and study, the chances of this happening naturally may be few. Learning experiences of this kind cannot be left to chance. The educational system must be designed to create opportunities for students to experience this kind of learning. With this and other realizations in mind, I began to sense that my calling was to be a teacher. I believed I could do better than many of my teachers had in designing and implementing instructional strategies.

To understand today's educational system fully, we must understand other theories that gave rise to it. As our country grew throughout the 20th century, mass production of goods and services was the principal means of satisfying people's needs. At one time, it was thought that people management would be the same in any organization. This idea was expressed by Frederick Taylor, but there were corollaries to it.

THE INDUSTRIAL MODEL

Believing that workers are motivated mainly by economic considerations, Taylor advocated "scientific management" of factory production. This method was characterized by time-and-motion studies, interchangeable parts, and standard processes, among other scientific and efficiency techniques (Drucker, 1968). Many of Taylor's ideas resulted in such practices as task limits, standard working conditions, merit pay, loss of remuneration in case of failure, division of labor, limited span of control, and homogeneity of positions. People were perceived as extensions of the machines they operated, and it was thought they could be controlled solely by external forces in the production process.

14

As the schools developed during this time in our nation's history, the "Industrial Model" became the design of choice for educators.

K-1-2-3-4-5-6-7-8-9-10-11-12 =

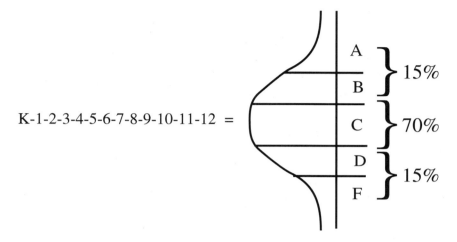

Figure 2.1
Industrial Model Applied to Grading in Education

Many industrial "efficiency concepts" were adopted and given a home in school systems. The assembly-line mentality is evidenced in the notion of management from the top, the practice of grade-level grouping, standard achievement-level expectations, the sorting and labeling of children, competition within and among students for grades, and evaluation schemes that determine "winners" and "losers." These terms may not always be used openly, but the idea that some students will succeed and others will fail is a felt theme in many school programs.

THE SPECIFICATION LIMITS MODEL

Along with the Industrial Model of managing people to achieve production efficiency, the Specification Limits Model became the method of determining acceptability of performance. Engineers chose close tolerances in the size and quality of workmanship in moving parts to ensure that manufactured devices would work, to standardize the assembly process, and to smooth the flow of production. The Specification Limits Model, with its upper and lower limits of acceptable performance, was a standard feature of industry almost from the start. It allowed different manufacturing processes to come together within acceptable degrees of craftsmanship to result in products that worked.

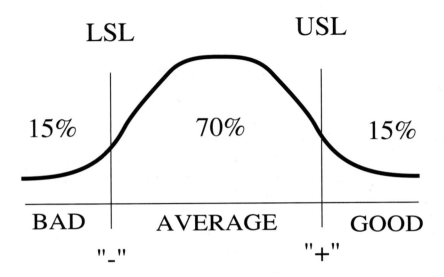

LSL   **USL**

15%   70%   15%

BAD   AVERAGE   GOOD

"–"   "+"

(lower specification limit)   (upper specification limit)

Figure 2.2
Specifications Limits Model

This notion of specification limits became a part of the Industrial Model for schools. Educators distorted the concept of normal distribution of behavior by imposing specification limits in order to sort, label, and rank people in the learning system. They came to expect a lower 15 percent and an upper 15 percent of performance everywhere they looked. We see this "Taylor thinking" played out in the classification of special needs, the awarding of honors, grading policies, selection of students for special programs, targeted instructional strategies—all of which result in stratification and rating of learners regardless of age.

THE COMPETITIVE MODEL

Early in our history, the only way workers gained a voice in the "management-labor" discussion was to form a union and, if necessary, strike to force supervisors and managers to pay attention to employee needs. The Competitive Model is thus inherent in the industrial fabric of this country. "Owners" and their "workers" are often polarized. Other manifestations of competition in the manufacturing realm include workers competing for merit salaries, interdivisional quests for earnings based on production, and struggles among sales people for new clients and bonus pay. The list goes on.

Today, we see results of the Competitive Model—many businesses forced out of existence because managers and workers refuse to cooperate. People on both sides of this schism can be at fault. Labor demands may be too high. Management greed, for both power and material gain, can also be high. Parties on both sides bargain out of self-interest and care little about the needs and concerns of those on the other side. In this kind of relationship, everyone loses. The Competitive Model has been transferred into the schooling process in many forms. The grade and recognition race begins in elementary school. Students compete for various awards, ribbons, certificates, and limited numbers of honors. Competition is built into the classrooms through time limits on exams, limits on the number of top grades given, and pressure placed on learners, subtle or otherwise, to become the best. The idea of students cooperating in the process and helping each other learn is being introduced in schools, but widespread acceptance of it is slow in coming, and sometimes it is interpreted as cheating.

The combined effect of these thinking and planning models—Industrial, Specification Limits, and Competitive—has sown seeds of destruction. The assumptions and approaches involved limit learners' intrinsic motivation and the cooperative atmosphere needed for enhancement of self-esteem as well as intellectual and creative development.

CONCERNS NOTED EARLY

Elton Mayo and F. J. Roethlisberger challenged much of early thinking in education because of studies done at Western Electric's Hawthorne Plant in Cicero, Illinois, during the late 1920s and early 1930s. These studies showed that organizations should be viewed as social systems and that "social pressure" influences people's behavior more than rules do. They suggested that management should adopt participative leadership styles and pay attention to the social conditions in which people work

(Hellriegel, Slocum, and Woodman, 1992). The human relations priority reflected in these examinations tempered the prevailing emphasis on order and discipline in organizational structures.

These and similar studies, making their way into boardrooms and upper management offices in the 1960s and 1970s, brought about some positive change in the work realm. Yet the Industrial Model of high control, limited focus, low integration, and "Theory X" (the notion that people fundamentally dislike work, are not willing to work hard, need to be controlled, and tend to avoid responsibility) was still firmly in place in business and industry. It was also reflected in schools.

Douglas McGregor had another idea. His "Theory Y" assumed that, in general, people are not lazy, that they want to contribute and take responsibility, and that they take pleasure in work when they are given the resources to complete tasks they are given (McGregor, 1985).

Another major theory, which we know today as the "Behavioral Objectives" approach to management, was introduced in the 1960s and 1970s as a way of improving on the Industrial Model. The emphasis in this approach was on objectives, results, and the so-called "bottom line." The methods through which desired goals might be effectively met were largely ignored. Many industrialists and business people quickly assimilated this manner of thinking, and the schools were brought along for the ride.

Throughout these decades, and to a certain extent in the 1980s, educators believed that setting clear goals and objectives, holding people accountable, and rating and ranking people would improve educational output. It did not happen! In fact, in 1983 the *Nation at Risk* report warned that mediocrity in the schools was undermining America's global competitiveness. In 1991, Deputy Secretary of Education David Kearns declared that more than half of the young people in America were unable to contribute to society in a meaningful way after graduating from high school (Deming Library, 1991).

RESPONSE TO THE DOWNWARD SLIDE

In the 1980s, the concept of viewing an organization as a system emerged. This idea is not new, but it seemed to be a new discovery in the

United States. As viewed by corporate managers, the system concept is still limited to the notion of communicating with workers in ways that emphasize goals and the ever-present bottom line. Management by objectives in a systems approach still tends to involve ranking and rating of people and holding them accountable for system results. In certain situations, this approach minimizes the value of individuals for the sake of system efficiency. This mindset is not much different from the Taylor model, except that it is applied in higher levels of technology.

BACK TO THE FUTURE

In the long term in both business and education, misguided and outmoded models of thinking have resulted in loss. The intrinsic value of people has been discounted. Human potential is far from being realized. It is time for educators and others connected with schools to make a change. Our task is to turn the system into one that expands students' horizons and helps them develop attitudes, skills, and ways of relating to people that will lead them to be productive, responsible, and fulfilled in life. The system must also reward excellence and make the learning process a joy. Dr. Deming's systematic application of continual improvement is the key to quality in transforming the educational system. Leadership creates system understanding and the environment for predicting results. The aim of this new philosophy is continual improvement.

REFERENCES

Deming Library (1991). Videotape, XVI.

Drucker, P. (1968). *The age of discontinuity.* New York: Harper & Row.

Hellriegel, D., Slocum, J., and Woodman, R. (1992). *Organizational behavior* (6th ed.). St. Paul, MN: West Publishing.

McGregor, D.M. (1985). *The human side of the enterprise* (2d ed.). New York: McGraw-Hill.

p a r t

2

The Road We Should Travel

People are asking for better schools, with no clear idea how to improve education, nor even how to define improvement of education.

W. Edwards Deming

CHAPTER 3

SYSTEM AND QUALITY
KEYS TO TRANSFORMATION

The Deming concept of quality is best explained by putting it into a system context. A system is a network of functions, elements, and processes within an organization, all of which work together to achieve the organization's aim. Functions are tasks performed by various work units, which can be individual people or groups. Functions in an educational system include curriculum, instruction, administration, guidance, evaluation, supervision, and transportation. Elements are parts of functions. For example, elements of the transportation function within a school system include buses, mechanics, drivers, students, and parents who see that their children are waiting at stops on time. A function such as school bus transportation can be thought of as a system of its own within the larger entity of a school system. A process is a series of steps that a particular work unit takes to complete a task. Since the ordering of instructional materials involves clearly defined procedures, it is considered a process. A system can be small and relatively simple. It can be large and complex. The basic model of a system is demonstrated by the following diagram.

SYSTEM TRANSFORMATION

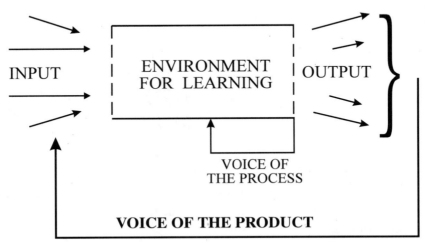

Figure 3.1
Voices of Internal and External Clients Receiving Services
(Source: Scherkenbach, 1991)

THE SYSTEM-QUALITY INTERFACE

System dynamics and quality are inextricably linked. A system can exist independently of quality, but quality cannot exist outside of a system. This truth was strongly impressed on me when I worked with Dr. William Hitzmen, superintendent of a suburban school district near Chicago, in developing a sequential and integrated district curriculum. For the first time, educators at all grade levels and in all schools in that district understood the big picture. They recognized their interrelationships and the curricular interdependency throughout the system. Teachers and other professional staff were not the only players, however. Students, parents, administrators, and local residents were all included in the design and development process. The networking system that evolved included communication linkages, new organizational structures, staff development programs, parent conferences, community relations activities, public relations programs, school board committees,

24

and school-business partnerships. Establishment of this broader community of interest was a first step in the direction of improving quality in the system.

THE ROLE OF LEADERSHIP IN SYSTEM CHANGE

Leaders are responsible for system improvements. No one else can make them. People working in an organization can recommend new approaches, but they cannot implement them except in their individual work areas, which may be limited. Leaders define the larger system and clarify its aim. Good leaders understand that for a system to function optimally, the people working in it need to be valued above all else. Effective leaders know that the combined influence of talented people working together creates an atmosphere in which the system can be continually improved. Think of it this way . . .

PEOPLE WORK IN A SYSTEM.

LEADERS WORK ON THE SYSTEM.

EVERYONE WORKS TOWARD CONTINUAL IMPROVEMENT OF THE SYSTEM TO ACHIEVE THE AIM.

People moving through a system in which these principles are in effect gain in knowledge and experience, deriving satisfaction from their work and becoming ever more valuable to the organization. As they benefit from the system, they help improve it. This is why leaders need a system perspective. That is, they must keep track of every major component in the system and how it functions to achieve the system aim. In education, this means keeping individual students, teachers, support people, administrators, parents, and members of the community in mind as well as the various groupings of these participants in the process. It means seeing how parts of the whole mix and multiply in the effort to provide learning opportunities and impetus for improvement. Maintaining a system-wide view involves mental and relational processes that leaders either learn or are encouraged to initiate. These are some of the components of an educational system:

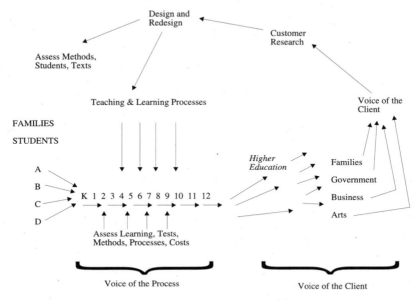

Figure 3.2
Viewing the "System" in an Extended Manner
Sources: Leonard (1991), Moen (1989), Scherkenbach (1991)

IDENTIFYING MAJOR SYSTEM COMPONENTS

Systems must be managed. Left to themselves, they will become dysfunctional. Also, if a system is not managed, the role of persons or groups within it may not be clear, and their relationships with other people and groups, as well as with the system as a whole, may not be understood. When this happens, the system cannot develop to its capacity. So it is important that leaders know the function of each major component of the system for which they are responsible. The instructional system in education, for example, is supposed to enable each learner to make the next moves in his or her learning program. If it is to meet student needs effectively, an instructional program must include upstream diagnosis—that is, analysis of individual learning capabilities made early enough in the school experience to provide for individual differences in instructional methods. When this does not happen, students can get lost in the shuffle, and if they do, the system has failed.

26

CLARIFYING THE AIM

Overall objectives give purpose and meaning to everyone's efforts, but if the aims of the system are not understood by each participant in the workplace, the system loses effectiveness. If workers operate in a vacuum, bent on meeting their own needs only, the system breaks down. This frequently happens in traditional school systems. The following chart indicates that how one views evaluation, departmental structure, and the instructional process determines loss or gain in the educational process.

	Loss	**Gain**
Evaluation of student performance	Using grades merely to classify learners.	Using gradeless evaluations based on valid performance criteria to help students meet objectives that have real-world relevance.
Departmentalization of subject matter	Limiting and controlling the curriculum so it stays within traditional boundaries.	Integrating learning experiences wtihin the subject matter areas and across other disciplinary lines so that the bigger picture of knowledge and individual growth comes into focus.
The instructional process	Involving a single method.	Utilizing many and varied approaches.

ORGANIZING INTERNAL AND EXTERNAL RELATIONSHIPS

All components of a system are interdependent to some degree. Any action on the part of one has an impact on the whole system. The role of administrators is to help teachers and support personnel extend their influence beyond the groups in which they work on a day-to-day basis. Ideally, everyone in the system is expanding his or her contacts to seek opportunities for system improvement, and everyone is making gains on the challenges the system faces.

A mobile hanging over a baby's crib is an excellent picture of what happens. As the baby touches one element in the mobile, others are set in motion, and the entire structure starts reacting. The interdependency of the parts of the mobile is clear, as is the reason for change—someone with an idea of what can happen is making movements that affect the entire system.

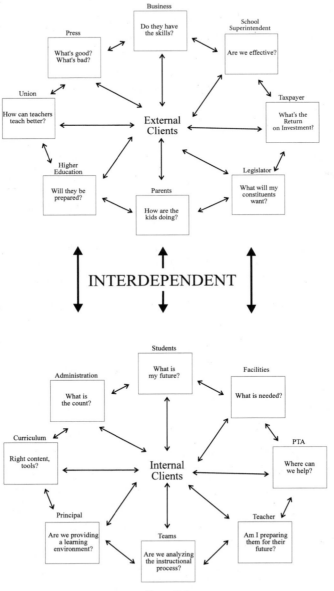

Figure 3.3
Interdependency of External and Internal Clients

ANALYZING THE VARIOUS CLIENTS

Learning is the product of the educational system. The product is delivered through the instructional system. It is through this instructional context that the internal and external clients interact to cause learning. The primary clients of the instructional process are the people who use the process, benefit from the process, and apply the capacity gained as a result of the process.

The people who use the instructional process are all the clients who create the learning environment that enables learning. The learning environment consists of many inputs: teachers, teaching strategies, materials, facilities, different media, attitudes of various interest groups, learner readiness, and a host of others. The student is the main benefactor of the instructional process. However, everyone who is involved in the continual improvement of the process learns and gains from the process. Therefore, the benefactor and user work together to optimize the system.

The end users of the application of the instructional process are the external clients, who benefit from the capacity that is improved through the students' learning. The interdependence of the various components define the schooling process: the primary users (staff), the benefactors (students), and the value-added student capacity. The educational process is defined by extending beyond the schooling process in both directions by adding the learning-environment providers and the student-capacity users.

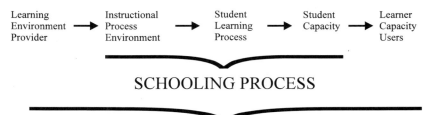

SCHOOLING PROCESS

EDUCATION PROCESS

Figure 3.4
Schooling and Educational Processes

The clients of the instructional process may not be the people who provide the financial support for the services. The legislature and/or the parent who provides the funds for the children's educational programs are not the clients of the services being provided. Understanding the various clients within a system is not easy. Also, identifying and nurturing the suppliers of the system are critical to the maintenance of the support of the system. Board members, legislatures, business partners, parents, community organizations, taxpayers, and other groups and individuals are suppliers who support the educational system. Families are suppliers of the student population for the educational system. Working with these suppliers may determine the conditions of the system.

It is critical to analyze the types of clients in the system and to understand their relationships to the achievement of the aim. All must work together to improve the instructional system and achieve the aim: creating a higher capacity for everyone!

LISTENING

To know whether improvements in the system are being made, leaders must have a constant flow of information from processes within it. Without this feedback, they may allow the system to drift in directions that are not consistent with the overall aim. Internal analysis is one aspect of continual improvement. The feedback, which can be thought of as the "voice" of the process, is provided at the instructional or building level, where the system's primary internal "clients" are its students. However, leaders need to be sensitive to another kind of feedback—the collective responses of external customers from industry, government and education. In educational systems, whoever receives school services needs to be working with school personnel to provide feedback on expectations that are either met or unmet. A school's outside customers include students' families and area residents, including employers, technical or vocational training schools, colleges and universities, and the various branches of military service. These external users of the educational product have a "voice" as well. Without the cooperation of clients inside the system and outside it, a crucial ingredient in system improvement is missing.

ENCOURAGING TEAMWORK

In general, educational leaders have not been taught how to implement assurances of quality into their systems. This is why productivity has lagged. Simply adding money does not necessarily improve the situation. In fact, if no method for continual improvement is in place, the infusion of money can cause additional waste. System improvement needs to be the constant focus of discussion, and there needs to be cooperation at all levels. The system structure as it is designed in most situations does determine many of the results. Traditional performance review does not encourage cooperation and trust within the system. To facilitate this, school administrators must eliminate performance reviews that hold *individuals* accountable for the results of the system. If teachers and other school personnel are continually evaluated as individuals, they will always feel that they are on trial, and what is desperately needed—a system check—may never be undertaken. In an atmosphere of collaboration, most people will enjoy improving their performance. However, if they are forced to compete with each other for advancement or recognition, the system fails and people lose. Only leaders can create the right atmosphere by changing the system.

MAKING NEW CONNECTIONS

Cross-functional integration of ideas is crucial. When people of different backgrounds and interests work harmoniously, the results of their interactions are synergistic (greater than the sum of individual efforts), and as energy of this kind builds within a system, new and better ways to do everything result. Productivity increases. Experimentation and innovation begin to flourish. There is room to breathe, take pride in the work being done, and have fun. An example of this from industry is the rapid success of the Ford Taurus and Toyota Lexus. In those car-manufacturing projects, a largely unprecedented spirit of cooperation among people in different departments resulted in single-minded focus on quality.

This is why interdisciplinary teaching teams are essential. Groups composed of educators who have different vantage points can mine a subject for deeper veins of insight than can teachers with similar viewpoints working in isolation. Interdisciplinary teaching teams can also determine efficient learning processes for desired outcomes. When teachers operate in self-contained units defined by subject matter, they may have good results in a narrow sphere, but they can inadvertently compromise student learning in other areas.

There are two ways in which teaching staffs can work together. One is "vertical integration." Secondary math teachers coming together for planning purposes is an example of vertical integration. As a means of enhancing communication, educators meeting in such configurations must ignore individual position titles. "Horizontal integration," on the other hand, draws together specialists at a specified level—all third-grade teachers or all teachers of high school freshmen, for instance. Secondary math and science teachers meeting together is an example of horizontal integration with an interdisciplinary dimension. If humanities teachers are added to the mix, many additional integrations of subject matter are possible. Professional groupings of this nature can address the way a concept, skill, or learning process manifests itself in different subject areas at a given phase of student development. In all forms of integration—horizontal, vertical, and multidisciplinary—different interests must be blended with the needs and priorities of various clients in mind. When connections like these are being made, the system is moving toward optimization for everyone, and momentum of this kind is crucial in developing overall system quality.

WHAT QUALITY IS

As Deming explained, the achievement of continual improvement of each function, element, and process determines quality. It is an attitude and motivating force that should permeate an organization. It is itself a process and, at the same time, an attribute of the end product. As a process, quality is continual improvement. When an organization has a good product, such as well-schooled students leaving an educational system to take responsible positions in society, it has a sense of identity and purpose and a reputation for quality. It produces individual satisfaction as well. In an organization in which quality is a paramount concern, everyone wins. There are no losers. This means everyone involved is improving in performance and gaining in self-worth, and the sum total of positive individual change is organizational improvement.

The idea of continual improvement creates opportunities for meaningful integration of functions, elements, and processes within a system, and, when these components are combined in new and better ways, the people involved understand their interdependency. They can also perceive time as an ally, realizing that personal improvement and process refinement are lifelong pursuits. Although work can and usually does involve deadlines, the most significant pressures felt by those working in this system do not come from the clock or calendar but from the common desire to satisfy the needs of clients—to meet their expectations and eventually exceed them.

Ideally, people entering an education system at any level of participation add value to themselves and to the system as a whole. The system should increase the capabilities of students, teachers, administrators, parents, and members of the community. If it does so, the system itself improves, for almost everyone involved realizes the need to work for system improvement and accepts that responsibility. Once it catches on, the continual improvement philosophy enables people in education to improve each instructional process, each administrative function, each budget analysis, each purchase of materials or supplies, each building use, each special service, each long-range plan, and each short-term strategy. The result is satisfied "customers."

Every component of the system (Figure 3.5) has value added to it by each of the other components in the system.

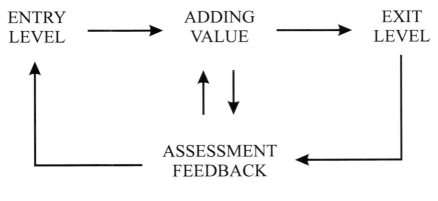

Figure 3.5
Adding Value to Win

Interdependence of each component of the system creates a need for everyone to work together for all to win.

Deming's idea of improvement consists of two important concepts. One is continual improvement of a system's *performance average* (statistical mean) around the target. The other is continual reduction of *system variation* around the target. If the system average improves and variation is reduced, everyone gains and the aim is eventually achieved. The figure below illustrates the first idea. The group is moving in the desired direction using academic achievement as an example.

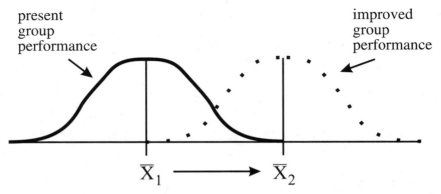

Figure 3.6
Normal Distribution Curve Showing Group Improvement

Figure 3.7 demonstrates the second idea, *reduction of variation* from performance improvement:

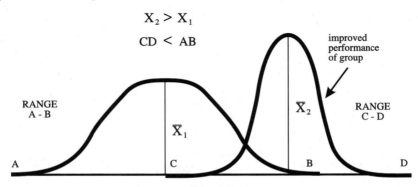

Figure 3.7
Normal Distribution Curve Showing Improvement and
Reduced Variation After the Improvement Intervention

34

VARIATION AFTER THE IMPROVEMENT INTERVENTION

A middle school at which I was principal exemplifies both ideas. In the first month of a school year there, I was approached by teachers who were concerned about slow growth and extensive skill variation among children in reading groups. When I asked how the groups were formed, the teachers said they had used standardized reading scores from the previous year. Realizing the amount of error in any standardized examination relative to individual achievement, I asked the teachers to give each student a reading inventory assessment. The teachers objected, for testing time would be extensive. They did not know how it could be accomplished in their busy schedule. I offered to release a staff reading specialist for this purpose. The process might take two months. Everyone wanted accurate information, so that approach was taken. Almost two months later, the results were available, and, with new information, teachers continually regrouped the children. In addition, reading instruction was scheduled for one hour at the same time for all grade levels in the school. Every teacher taught reading during this period, and students moved from group to group depending on the instructional skills needed, regardless of their age or grade level. They could be in a group for a week or as long as a month—whatever it took to help them acquire the skill they needed. No letter grades were given for learning advancement. No ranking of students was done, and students helped each other. The switch was successful. Reading skill improved everywhere. At year's end, the district gave a standard reading test. Even with the error factor considered, it was clear that students in this school had never gained so much in reading proficiency, either as a whole or individually, in one academic year—and the new groupings and approaches had been in place only from December through May of the following year.

This situation illustrates key concepts of the Deming philosophy: *improving the mean* and *reducing variation* in performance. Both processes involved gathering and interpreting reliable data. First, student reading abilities were accurately measured. Second, the instructional process was changed in such a way that student needs were addressed in a timely manner. Also, adjustments were continually made as students progressed. Students moved to whatever group better enhanced their learning and growth. With students in each group operating at close to the same capability (regardless of age or grade level), teachers could focus and maximize their efforts. The entire student population did better, and the gap between high and low achievers was narrowed.

What Quality Is Not

From these definitions and concrete examples, we can broaden the discussion to include popular but limited notions of organizational quality.

Quality Is Not Just Meeting Client Demands.

If an organization responds only to clients' perceived needs, it will be hard-pressed to stay in business. The only organizations that would survive are those whose funding is automatic, independent of what or how well they do. This may be why public schools have been able to ignore improvement for so many years. Any organization that wishes to advance must not only meet but exceed client needs. And clients often are not aware of all their needs. How many people asked for microwave ovens or mobile phones before these convenience-oriented products were created? Nevertheless, people learn quickly when advanced strategies and amazing products are made available to them. Likewise, to meet the constantly changing needs of this fast-paced century and the next one, schools must get beyond their current strategies. At the same time, school services must be given careful thought, for identified needs may not always be ones that should be filled. A child's need to walk across a busy street alone may not be safe without a helping hand from a parent.

Those who have the idea of service excellence either see or create opportunities to give clients what they would not necessarily expect or think to ask for—additional information, immediate responses, support, and being open to feedback. For example, as a middle school principal, I had an idea for improving communication between school and home. I created a conference process in which students themselves were expected to share information about their learning progress with their parents. Teachers were available to support students as they did this and to share additional information as needed. Academic achievement was the focus. No letter grades were involved. Following the conferences, written summaries were sent home. No student, teacher, parent, or other administrator in the district asked for this reporting process. As principal, I created and implemented it. Parents and students alike agreed that it was an excellent approach with many unanticipated benefits. Receiving more from their school system than they expected, they were pleasantly surprised.

QUALITY IS NOT SIMPLY A MATTER OF CLIENT PREFERENCES.

At times, quality is erroneously equated with preference. In purchasing a car, for example, we are told that leather is better than cloth for seat covers, so we may develop a preference for leather. Appropriate car-seat coverings may have more to do with geographic location and climate, however, than with perceived notions of quality. Some cloth seat covers last longer than leather coverings, and to some people, cloth covers feel better. We are led to believe that brand-name drug products are better than generic products. But if drug products of the same type are chemically identical, they are the same; it doesn't matter what name is on the container. We may sometimes prefer shopping for brand-name china in an expensive department store over going to a discount store that has the same pattern and plate at a lower price. Yet a brand-name china plate is the same whether it is sold at a boutique or a volume-buy warehouse. So you see, we are led to prefer many products on the basis of myths and misconceptions.

In education, too, preference may be confused with quality. Students and their parents may choose a particular school believing its instructional program is outstanding. However, one school may be as good as another, depending on individual needs, and a school may be excellent but not be preferred by all students. Those in public service need to realize that presenting a range of excellent alternatives is important. However, it is equally important not to confuse choice with quality.

QUALITY AND ADVANCED TECHNOLOGY ARE NOT EQUIVALENT.

Because technology is impressive, we tend to believe it improves quality of life—and in most instances it does. We may think more is better: more recording ability, more phone-message capability, more power in a motor, more fan speed, and so on. The key to using technology is understanding that it is a tool. If the aim is not achieved, it is not necessarily better to have more gadgets; in fact, they can make things worse. One example that comes to mind is the voice-mail system at a certain university. Everyone there thought it would be great to have. It would improve communication, student relations, and response time on many work-related inquiries. However, after one year, many people are not satisfied with the system. It is hard to find a human being to talk to. One wonders sometimes if human beings work at the university any longer. Students frequently have difficulty reaching professors, or professors cannot speak directly to a departmental secretary. When everyone is talking to everyone else's voice mail, the frustration level is high. The system is high-tech, yes, but it has diminished the quality of communication.

Educators are inclined to believe that technology will enhance learning. In reality, it may not. Technology can improve a process, but it does not affect learning. Students might use a calculator or a computer to complete an assignment, but understanding of a math problem or a written message cannot be attained through these devices. Many students can solve problems without computers and other modern equipment. Technology is important in that it saves time and labor, but it will not improve a process in and of itself. The quality of a process or system must be determined by the people who lead, manage, and work in the system. People are the most important element in any system, not the tools they use.

NUMERICAL STANDARDS ALONE HAVE LITTLE TO DO WITH QUALITY.

Educational communities at all levels are setting standards and quotas. The belief is that by setting a standard, people will meet it and system quality will improve. The fact is that setting standards can be a setback to educational progress. In one large metropolitan school system, it was decreed that no student would be allowed to move from eighth grade to high school without demonstrating the ability to read at the sixth-grade level. It was amazing how many students were able to improve their reading scores instantly. It was widely suspected that teachers taught directly to the tests and that scores were changed to meet the standard. A real problem remained, however. Many students still did not meet the standard. The problem was "solved" the following academic year by eliminating the policy. In another school in which student scores increased dramatically, it was determined that test reports were falsified. The investigation revealed that the principal's salary was dependent upon the student achievement levels.

Many state governments are setting standards for their school systems. Each school is assessed against a set expectation and then told whether that has been met. The question might be asked of the principal or superintendent, how might you raise the performance of your students on the state exams? Many creative strategies have been implemented. Teaching to the test is the most honorable. However, some administrators have kept certain students from taking the tests, omitted scores of certain students in reporting results, and misreported scores. Why? To save face in the community and do the job that is expected of them: meeting the standard.

Some educators have been led to believe that Management By Objective (MBO), Management By Results (MBR), Objective Based Education (OBE-1), Outcome Based Education (OBE-2), mastery learning, setting minimum standards—whatever is popular at the time—will improve learning. Using these management ideas, school leaders implement mass inspection systems with standardized tests. Meanwhile, society evaluates everyone in the educational system based on the results. The irony of setting numerical standards is that everyone is competing with everyone else to do better, yet everyone loses. All of these approaches elevate numbers to a position of importance, but they have nothing to do with system improvement.

Educators with the attitude of excellence create higher standards naturally through continual improvement of every process. When improvements are made on an ongoing basis and integrated with each other within a system, the final service or product is better than anything that could have been envisioned by focusing on individual components.

QUALITY IS NOT ACHIEVED BY MASS INSPECTION.

Mass inspection of student performance is an industry, and test results, among other things, become the basis for evaluating educational programs. Schools are ranked, needs are determined, and in some cases funds are allocated on the basis of test scores. Community pressure to achieve is extremely strong in high-achieving schools as well as low-achieving schools. Many "games" are played to ensure a higher ranking. How does all this relate to the true quality of education? It doesn't. Learning improvement, rather, could be assessed through individual sampling of the results of services being performed and by determining how well they line up with the system aim. This allows for an evaluation of the system. In most instances, mass measurements are a waste of time and money. You cannot increase the weight of a pig by placing it on a scale, but you can by feeding it more effectively. Giving a pig a better eating process or method is changing the system by which it grows.

QUALITY IS NOT NECESSARILY A RESULT OF HARD WORK.

It is often said that if people would just pay attention and concentrate more, the quality of their work would improve. But let's think about that. How many of us awoke this morning and planned to do things wrong today? Generally speaking, people want to do a good job at whatever they are doing. Many do not have the proper education, training, tools, equipment, or support systems to do well, but they do not actively wish to do poor work. Working hard in ill-conceived activities is unproductive at best, and it can be counterproductive. Working "smart" is more important than working hard. Knowing the purpose of tasks and how they relate to tasks elsewhere in the system is critical. When intelligent choices are being made on this basis, practically everyone comes to work willing to do a good job. When people know they are valued and are asked to analyze data as a way of improving the system (rather than always feeling that the focus is on personal performance), extrinsic pressures are removed, stronger internal motivation comes into play, and everyone begins to pull in the same direction.

INDIVIDUAL PERFORMANCE REVIEWS HAVE LITTLE EFFECT ON QUALITY.

Most educational administrators believe and are taught that personal accountability for teachers and others in the system is a good idea. But performance reviews, particularly annual assessments, assume that workers are totally responsible for the work they do. The process rarely recognizes interrelationships among workers. And administrators themselves are held accountable. Their salaries and tenure in their jobs depend on their achieving specific objectives. It sounds fair in theory. Are we not responsible for what happens in our work area? Suppose something does not go well at work because people on whom we depend do not do their jobs right. Are we not paid to solve such problems and get the job done? If a student gets a certain grade, shouldn't there be a ranking based on it, and isn't that ranking what the student deserves? Does it matter how grades are determined from class to class, teacher to teacher, course to course? Do grades mean anything to anybody?

As Deming saw it, grades and evaluations do not mean much. The results of these processes are more a reflection on the system than on individuals, and the results that really matter in education are a function of larger systems in which individual people play relatively small roles. So personal evaluation does little to produce quality. Indeed, almost everyone has felt the negative results of a performance evaluation. Even if only one item is adverse, the review is generally perceived as a negative message. Morale plummets. On a daily basis, the vast majority of students get the message that they are not good enough. Any grade of C or less is perceived as not good enough. How would you like to come to a place where you are told 85 percent of the time that you are not good enough? Constant negative feedback shuts people down. They don't want to think about how to make the system better, because they have to compete with those who are doing better than they are. They learn to "play the game" to get the best rating in a system of extrinsic rewards. This is a no-win situation.

QUALITY IS NOT ACHIEVED BY MERIT PAY.

In theory, organizational reward systems give everyone a chance to win, but in real life relatively few people come out on top. Consider grades. Using the "normal" distribution curve, only so many As can be given. How many students are going to offer to help other students do better? Students learn early in their school experience that they need to get the best grades, have the highest average, and get the highest rank. Winning at all costs is the driving force, and joy in the learning process is usually lost. Similarly, if a principal's salary is based on merit as assessed by student academic performance, why would that person want his or her staff to share teaching strategies with teachers in other schools for the sake of improving overall instruction in the district? It makes no sense to help other schools do better. Doing so may cost the principal a higher salary or eventually a job.

Fortunately, incentive pay is not often used in education. It can't produce quality. Incentive pay rewards the individual and rarely has anything to do with client service. A business analogy is valid. Many salespeople deliver or sell whatever produces the highest commission for them. From a business with educational products or services, a school might receive large quantities of unneeded items, unwanted services, superfluous copy machines, unwarranted repair jobs—all because commission is the incentive. Even salespeople in these situations can lose, however, for in the long run customers figure out that their real needs are not being met.

Also, most awards are given for outstanding performance. Yet few people can distinguish between normal variation in performance and exceptional performance. Although most performance variation results from the random interaction of many variables, we tend to reward variation as if it were unusual. (The difference between normal and special performance variation is discussed in Chapter 6, "Knowledge: Prediction That Leads to Improvement.") True quality in education comes about when educational leaders know the difference between common and special causes of performance variation in their teaching staffs. Recognizing people for "superior" results when these may be normal within any system could be detrimental to the work atmosphere, diminish cooperation, and decrease the overall quality of teaching.

QUALITY IS NOT NECESSARILY "SUCCESS."

In fact, quality may not be related to success at all if it is defined as a set achievement standard. A school can be successful, achieve high scores on standardized tests, and not be implementing a quality instructional program. Pressure for grades can be applied, learning processes neglected, exam results alone rewarded, people undervalued, and quality of instruction ignored. By the same token, a school committed to quality may not be "successful" on a test-score basis.

Two high schools in one of the large industrial states of our nation, both thought to be among the best, serve to demonstrate confusion of this kind. In one school, staff members were interested in creating integrated learners—that is, students who can apply knowledge gained in one subject area to situations that arise in other disciplines, making unusual connections and drawing fresh inferences. This educational aim was agreed upon by the entire school community after a year of dialogue and debate. The teaching staff then came up with conceptually integrated, multidimensional units of study. Students became involved in the process and helped write the curriculum. As these units were implemented, however, teachers recognized that the school's departmental structure was impeding progress. After a year of struggling with traditional disciplines in place, the staff removed the departmental structures that separated them, creating integrated instructional teams that could handle thematic units of study. Over a three-year period, students, faculty, administrators, parents, and area business people all believed this approach would be of long-term benefit to the school's academically talented students. However, S.A.T. scores declined during those three years. This gave school and community leaders major cause for reflection, but they decided to continue with the program and explain the lower scores to admission officers of the colleges to which students might apply. In addition, discussion with S.A.T. officials resulted in a reassessment of that organization's test questions. The S.A.T., it was determined, was not addressing the integrated analysis skills being taught in this high school. As of now, the school is continuing to refine its integrated learning curriculum. This is leadership!

Another prestigious school in the same state achieved outstanding S.A.T. scores and has no academically integrated curricular programming. Academic departments are isolated from one another, and all strive to protect their turf and power base. Courses are created to justify new positions or defend old ones. Teachers do not share instructional ideas or materials. Students achieve high scores, but can they think? Not necessarily. This is not leadership! In one school, test scores go down but students win. In another, the scores go up but students lose. Which is a "quality" school? Which is a "successful" school? As you can see, quality may be correlated with success in some instances, but quality may not cause success. The outcome depends on what is valued and how success is defined.

THE LEADERSHIP CHALLENGE

Misguided notions of quality, such as those examined in this discussion, can give educational leaders latitude to blame others when ideas don't work. Admittedly, quality is an elusive goal. It is what any organization or society decides it values enough to devote time, energy, and resources to making excellent. Everyone may not agree on what it is. And, while recipients of educational services may not always know what they want, they tend to recognize "quality" when they see it. School administrators need to keep in mind that quality is continual improvement of what is desirable—not being satisfied with what is merely acceptable. The quest for quality creates ever higher standards, and the values and improvement processes set in motion by this quest can be passed on from worker to worker, family to family, generation to generation, society to society. In educational terms, this means constantly improving systems at many levels: one-on-one interactions between students and teachers, school and district-wide communications, policy development, community relations, and legislative and governmental action on the state and national levels must be locked into each other. When this happens, there will be more effective interaction among groups of people who have vested interests in process improvement, and the resulting system innovation will better prepare students for life.

REFERENCES

Leonard, J.F. (1991). "Applying Deming's principles to our schools." *South Carolina Business*, 11, pp. 82-87.

Moen, R.D. (1989). "The Deming philosophy for improving the educational process." Paper presented to the Third Annual International Deming Users' Group Conference in Cincinnati, Ohio (8/22/89), pp. 1-24.

Scherkenbach, W.W. (1991). *Deming's road to continual improvement.* Knoxville, TN: SPC Press, p. 64.

The result [of educational transforma-tion] will in time be greater innovation and reward for everyone. There will be joy in work, joy in learning. Anyone who enjoys his work is a pleasure to work with. Everyone will win; no losers.

W. Edwards Deming

CHAPTER 4

SYSTEM OPTIMIZATION
EVERYONE WORKING AT FULL CAPACITY

As a young boy in the late 1940s, I lived with my uncle and his family on a farm in northern Wisconsin. Most farms in that area were from 80 to 120 acres, and oats were one of the main crops. Many families did not have running water in their homes. Some had no electricity. Despite the lack of these amenities, life was full of meaningful activities, and there was a real sense of community among the people. At harvest time, many farmers helped each other. A large threshing machine was set up on a farm, and neighboring farmers and their families came together to collect the oats.

While the men and boys worked in the fields, women and girls prepared noon meals. Within each of these spheres of activity, work was apportioned according to individual inclination and ability. Men and women and boys and girls could already perform well in the tasks they were assigned, or it was clear that they could learn to with experience. My job at this early age was to drive a tractor slowly as men loaded bundles of shocked oats onto a hay wagon. I made mistakes when I first tried this, of course, but I got better at it and eventually felt a lot of satisfaction in being a fully functioning participant in the work activities. Once the harvest was finished at a particular farm, the work team moved to the next farm, and so on—a process that continued for several weeks.

Looking back on that time, I can see that this way of life taught me a great deal. These farmers knew the value of teamwork. They worked together to achieve a common aim. They completed the harvest quickly, and the process was cost-effective for each family. This is what is meant by optimization of a system. Having lived this principle as a youth, I find it natural to apply it in my work in education.

Cultivating Human Capacity

I will be forever grateful to Dr. William Hitzmen for giving me a chance to implement many of the ideas Dr. Deming challenged educators to adopt. The suburban school district in Chicago in which I worked was like many others throughout the nation in the early 1970s. It had self-contained classroom structures in which teachers did their best independently. There was little working together on curriculum development or budget analysis and not much staff development, student learning analysis, criterion assessment, implementation of common learning objectives, or other elements of what would be thought of today as a progressive learning organization. Yet, in four years, the staff turned the system into a fully integrated cooperative enterprise, with all parties working to improve instructional processes for each child. Excitement was high, and the level of professional commitment was inspiring. Most features of what we might call the Cooperative Philosophy of Education, which are described in detail in chapters to come, were implemented. These included team planning for instruction, groupings that involved children of different ages, portfolio assessment of each student, a parent-student-teacher progress conference process that involved no letter grades, teacher control of instructional budget allocation, teacher interviews to recommend candidates for teaching positions that became available, and teacher representation on all school board committees.

And, as I have said, educators at all grade levels and in all schools in the system understood the district's "big picture" for the first time. We changed the system in the hope that everyone in the community would benefit. The system became a living, learning organization. We worked in a unified way, every person and team considering improvement of the whole while improving individual performance. We saw proof of the validity of the process in gains on standard exams at all levels, and the test results were all the more remarkable considering that enrollment doubled during this four-year period. This was a wonderful experience for all the staff and students involved.

PRINCIPLES FOR PROFOUND CHANGE

Despite previous movements and attempts at reform, many educators are still unsure about how to achieve excellence across the board. Fads of recent years have led people to tinker and tamper with the system, but few trends have provided a strong enough challenge to preconceived notions for total system transformation to take place. Profound change is a process in which the educational system begins to

- Affirm the value of each person.

- Develop and enhance individual talent.

- Encourage creative thinking and problem solving.

- Improve the quality of life for each person and for society.

- Increase the challenge in and enjoyment of learning.

Each component of the system must be assessed for the degree to which it adds to or detracts from the aim, which is to help students realize their learning capacity. All shareholders in schools are to gain from the system, and the system is to benefit from the interaction among shareholders. In other words, where we sow quality methods, we reap improved results. However, for the system to be its best, everyone involved must understand and support the basic aim and "buy into" the continual improvement philosophy. Otherwise, people cannot do their jobs properly.

A school program can be difficult to optimize, because competition—an idea at odds with teamwork—tends to be deeply ingrained in our nation's thinking. Collaborative learning among students is at times considered a threat—an opportunity for cheating. Learning, however, is a process in which everyone must make gains. If one person fails to learn, all lose. Frankly, students can be of tremendous help to each other. Also, if educators wish to build trust with parents and students, they must be honest about what is expected academically and forthright in sharing the indicators of student performance. Then, working together, everyone involved can devote energy to improving the learning process. Teachers who are not committed to academic excellence set up situations that amount to cheating, for other shareholders in the system are then being deprived of the best use of time, money, and human resources.

When individuals or groups within a system lose their focus on the aim, the whole system suffers. A classic example of this occurred in recent years with the Sears Automotive Repair Division, in which mechanics were traditionally paid on a commission basis. It was discovered that customers were being overcharged and "repairs" were being made on items that did not need to be fixed. Why? The answer is obvious. The quest for money was driving the daily decision making. Mechanics and their supervisors were oblivious to Sears' reputation with the buying public. This was a classic case of sub-optimization. The system was working at far less than its potential and actually working to the customers' detriment. As this knowledge became public, Sears removed the incentive pay system and replaced it with set salaries. Customer service again was the focus.

As a new principal, I saw a similar situation. During my first year, I formed a new team of teachers who were to decide what instructional materials to purchase. In prior years, teachers would list their requests and submit them to the principal, who would then decide how the money was spent. Teachers would eventually receive some of the supplies they needed. I believed that teachers should know the process involved and make the final decisions. As teaching leaders were presenting their budget requests to this instructional-materials planning team, the school librarian stated that a certain item being requested, a $600 tape set, was already in the library. The tapes had been ordered previously by another team and were not often used—but they were there in the school. The planning team was taken by surprise, but because team requests were being considered in a new system of open communication, the teachers were able to avoid a purchase that would have been a waste of money. As effective use of instructional funds became a priority to the staff in this way, teachers became more willing to share materials and to pool budgeted money to make intelligent purchases of new equipment and supplies. Everyone knew where the funds were going. There was no mystery, no disparaging commentary, no interdepartmental gamesmanship. All concerned benefited because the budget process was designed to optimize the instructional materials purchasing system.

Transforming of the Educational System

As improvements of this kind are made in educational systems, a new wholeness starts to emerge, and levels of performance of staff members and students may go beyond anyone's expectation. People see themselves as part of a pattern that is working because they are operating at full capacity along with others who are doing the same. They realize that well-crafted interrelationships are responsible for up to 98 percent of system results in student learning. Dr. Deming predicted this. In 1989, in Osaka, Japan, he declared that educational transformation would involve a new system of reward. "The aim will be to unleash the power of human resource contained in intrinsic motivation," he said. "In place of competition for high rating, high grades, to be Number 1, there will be cooperation between and among people in grade levels, departments, subject areas, schools and throughout the community. The result will in time be greater innovation and reward for everyone. There will be joy in work, joy in learning. Anyone who enjoys his work is a pleasure to work with. Everyone will win; no losers" (Deming, 1989).

I believe it is important to highlight the capacities involved by contrasting specific attributes of present school systems (or at least what tends to be the case) with what the Deming philosophy suggests is both desirable and possible to achieve. Here are some examples.

Traditional School System:

Excellent instruction is thought of only in terms of how it increases costs.

Transformed School System:

Excellent instruction is considered an investment because it increases the value of money spent. A multiplier effect makes long-term returns on the investment substantial and reduces costs in the future.

Initially, our schools taught reading, math, and other subjects as discrete subjects, and materials were purchased to support each subject area independently. As we rethought the need for student learning as an integrated process with many dimensions, the thematic design of curriculum became a major priority. Much staff time and effort was spent in designing thematic units of study. Units were developed and taught as the school year advanced. In this context, reassessment of instructional materials was common, and new materials were selected on the basis of multiple use from multiple subject perspectives. Existing materials were viewed more flexibly, and many from different levels were made available for the diverse student groupings. Most important, materials selection was based on instructional needs and objectives, not on theoretical grade-level projections from publishers or standardized test "norms." Teachers had to learn instructional strategies and student-assessment techniques, and they had to become familiar with learning-style variations. The investment benefited everyone—the staff, students, parents, the program, and system. Eventually, we spent less money on materials because we used what we bought efficiently and effectively in many applications.

Traditional School System:	**Transformed School System:**
Age determines grade-level placement and expectations of student performance.	Individual student learning progress leads to continual advancement, independent of age.

For most learning, the placement of children in age-level groups makes little sense. Determining children's capabilities and performance levels and putting them in appropriate instructional situations makes more sense. The account given in the previous chapter of remarkable reading improvement that resulted from accurate testing and restructuring of grade-level reading groups is a good illustration.

Traditional School System:	**Transformed School System:**
Much time and energy goes into remediation, reworking, and retention.	With multi-age grouping, there is more tolerance of variation in skill development and a stronger focus on variations that are significant and require attention—as well as on those that are considered normal.

Children differ in how they learn and in the rate at which they progress, so instructional grouping is best done on the basis of individual needs. The reading-skill groups mentioned earlier often had three age levels of children, and the groups were constantly changing from week to week.

Traditional School System:

Students are graded, ranked, and labeled on the basis of that rank.

Transformed School System:

All students receive encouragement and help, and their advancement is based on accurate assessment of knowledge, understanding, and skill acquired with respect to specific criteria. The sense of "low group" or "high achiever" or "average student" that pervades most classroom situations is considered inappropriate.

Children should not compete against each other in learning. Performance standards or expectations should be clarified, and these should be the measure of advancement, but grading, ranking, and labeling students is a process unrelated to learning. A grade is a score. A score is a number. A number is a number. In most instances, it does not represent learning!

Traditional School System:

The Carnegie unit of seat time is considered important in determining instructional credit.

Transformed School System:

Teachers and students work together to assess learning levels. Teachers provide feedback and help students learn and grow. Credit received is a function of knowledge attained and skills acquired.

It is meaningless to equate seat time with learning. Learning assessment and feedback, on the other hand, enable teachers and students to understand what progress is being made and identify what needs to be improved.

Traditional School System:

Instruction is usually cyclic. Teachers cover content and skill areas, then test and grade, then repeat the pattern.

Transformed School System:

Teachers continually assess student progress and continually reassess instructional techniques for their applicability to individual learners. Learning activities are much less predictable.

The traditional approach is to teach, test, and grade, with little adaptation to changing realities. The new way is to teach, test, identify areas needing improvement, then teach again, trying new approaches. Continual improvement in the teaching process is recognized as the only way to meet and exceed expectations. Students are active participants in the feedback process to help the teacher know how instruction can be improved.

Traditional School System:

Subject matter is covered in separate courses.

Transformed School System:

The curriculum is thematically integrated, and learning projects that require interdisciplinary research and thinking are numerous.

Courses of study must demonstrate the real-life interdependency between subject areas. Math, science, social studies, reading, writing, art, technology, and many other spheres of knowledge must be combined in units of study. If this is not done, many students will not learn to make mental integrations on their own. Critical-thinking skills must be developed because they are needed in life. They do not come about by accident or simply as students grow older. We must create smarter people, not just older and more experienced people.

Traditional School System:

The general attitude is that instructional processes can be improved without the help of consultants. No system change and no input from students are needed.

Transformed School System:

The instructional process is in continual flux in the direction of improvement. Students and teachers work together to assess learning progress. The need for perspective and assistance from resource persons outside the system is recognized and welcomed.

No system improves without outside influences to challenge it. People with new information and ideas who are not normally a part of the school process should be invited to make suggestions and participate in instruction. Knowledge from outside the system can be stimulating and beneficial. Most challenge and change comes from outside the system.

Traditional School System:

Quotas and numerical goals drive the program.

Transformed School System:

The desire for continual improvement in instruction and elsewhere in the system drives the program.

Quotas and numerical goals, standards, numerical objectives, grades, rankings, and awards are based on the idea that stratification is unavoidable. But inevitably, they destroy the spirit of learning. If the focus is on the number, the grade, or the reward, few people in the situation are considering the process, which is more important. Improvement for everyone by improving the process of instruction is the real issue. All participants—students especially—are crucial to the instructional improvement process.

Traditional School System:

Fear and merit are motivations for learning and creative teaching.

Transformed School System:

Fear and merit systems have no place in the motivation of people involved in education. Joy in the process of learning and satisfaction in the results of learning are what transform people and the educational system.

Fear does not inspire people to do the right thing the right way. It merely gets them to do what it takes to keep their job or get their grade. It prevents people from trying new ways to improve the system. Fear makes people play it safe. It results in achievement at the lowest possible levels.

Traditional School System:

Administrators tend to believe teachers are sharper and more motivated when they do not have secure positions.

Transformed School System:

Administrators hire good teachers and do all they can to make them feel secure in their positions. In this atmosphere, teachers work hard, take risks, and become far more creative than they otherwise would.

Insecurity on the job is the best way to *prevent* people from improving themselves and the system. Teachers and students will not take risks in new ventures if they are afraid of being fired or downgraded. Failure causes closure!

Traditional School System:

Much of what students have in assignments is busy work and does not stimulate higher levels of thinking.

Transformed School System:

Students receive challenging, thoughtful assignments that are tied directly to assessment criteria. The amount of work done is less important than the quality of learning, experiences, and the results obtained.

Quality assignments are preferable to an emphasis on quantity of work. Assignments should be valuable to the student and create a favorable learning environment as well. Writing a book is an example. In doing this, students can learn much about language structure and the writing process, and about appropriate grammar, punctuation, and the nature of working. The result can be a valued piece of work that lasts a lifetime.

Traditional School System:

Students are motivated by extrinsic rewards.

Transformed School System:

Students are motivated by enjoyment of learning, satisfaction in doing the work well, and being recognized as unique persons who have important contributions to make.

The completion of valuable assignments gives satisfaction to both students and teachers. No amount of money or letter-grade reinforcement can take the place of the inner rewards that come from work that is done well and is meaningful to the student.

Traditional School System:

Classroom control is needed for learning to occur.

Transformed School System:

Mutual respect between teachers and students creates a good atmosphere for learning.

When students and teachers have the same objective—to create and maintain an environment in which learning is enjoyable and of obvious benefit—control is not a factor because it does not become an issue. As a school principal, I was once summoned to the cafeteria because of an emergency situation. An 11-year-old student was holding another student up against a wall at knifepoint. When I entered the area, I cleared the cafeteria so the only people remaining were the two boys, a teacher, and myself. After twenty minutes of discussion, the boy removed the knife from the other boy's throat and handed it to me. After school that day, I met with both boys' parents, their primary teacher, and other key people. I urged the whole group to consider what would be the best action to take for everyone in the long run as well as in the short run. The conclusion we came to was that the student would be under the direct supervision of the primary teacher every minute while in school but would not be suspended. All agreed with the action and understood the aim of having everyone gain over time. On another occasion, a student was found lying on the floor in the gymnasium locker area. The school nurse and I were summoned. The nurse quickly determined that the student had taken drugs but was not in any physical danger. We called the parents, discussed the issue, arranged for counseling, and worked with the family. The student was not suspended from school, and the family became closer.

At times, suspension is necessary. However, a policy of "zero tolerance" toward discipline problems in the school is not a good solution. It will only make things worse and be more costly. It will not improve the system. In both of the situations I have described, we had no further incidents of negative behavior. The willingness to care and trust that the students would follow through with their commitment to cooperate did allow everyone involved to win.

Traditional School System:

The teacher is G.O.D. (Giver of Directions)

Transformed School System:

The teacher is a facilitator of learning.

When cooperation out of respect for one another exists, the instructional process can be a partnership. Teachers help students grow and develop in ways they need to, and students help teachers see ways of improving their instructional methods. Positive change is possible and, ideally, perpetual.

Traditional School System:

Students read textbooks and complete assignments in workbooks.

Transformed School System:

Student work that is original and full of application to life develops naturally from group explorations in multidisciplined content areas and from intriguing questions posed by both students and teachers.

Textbooks and other instructional materials should engender and support student-teacher interaction. The materials themselves, however, should not be centerpieces in the process. Learning objectives, not materials, are the focal points. Life applications, special projects, and integrated activities to achieve curricular objectives should move the program forward. Materials change from year to year if teachers treat them as the means to achieve learning, not the object of learning itself.

Traditional School System:

Lectures are the main feature in the instructional process.

Transformed School System:

In addition to listening to lectures and taking notes, students learn by doing special projects on their own and participating in group work that involves stimulating assignments.

While the lecture is a valid teaching method, it is often too passive for many students. More active modes of instruction need to be utilized in the classroom. It is through interaction that students come alive and become involved in learning.

Traditional School System:

Evaluation is based on individual effort and achievement.

Transformed School System:

Student performance is partly an individual matter, but the ability to work well with others is also valued.

If students are individually evaluated, graded, rated, ranked, and performance-reviewed, they will not see the need to work well with others. Unless they happen to be high achievers, they will protect themselves, play it safe, and do the minimum in order not to be noticed. Evaluation of the system is critical. Teachers and students must feel free to improve it. If they are continually graded, they will probably hesitate to make suggestions. A spirit of cooperation is needed.

Traditional School System:

The performance of both teachers and students is generally tied to test scores, and often only the best are rewarded.

Transformed School System:

A wide variety of student interests and abilities is considered normal, and individual student needs are analyzed to determine whether they are common or require special attention. Teacher assessments follow the same principle. In a supportive environment, students and teachers alike receive the encouragement they need to improve.

There is normal variation in student performance. Only when students can be identified as special cases of concern can special help be made available to prevent learning losses. Early identification of significant individual deficits can put lagging students on their feet and keep them in school. The same is true of teachers.

Traditional School System:

Teachers often work independently, receiving little support from peers in improving instructional techniques.

Transformed School System:

Teachers assess each other's needs in a mutually supportive way and work together to improve the quality of instruction in all their classrooms and buildings and district-wide.

Staff cooperation and mentoring can result when teachers feel comfortable discussing their needs with each other. When teachers are continually trying to improve their service, the entire program—curriculum, instruction, materials, the learning process, and classroom environment—benefits. Everyone in the school works to help others.

Traditional School System:

Students are thought of merely as receivers of instruction, with little to say about how teaching strategies can be improved.

Transformed School System:

Students are considered an important resource in program improvement.

If continual improvement is the aim of the system, students can no longer be treated as passive participants. They are partners in the improvement process and beneficiaries of it.

Traditional School System:

Final exams and standardized tests determine student grades in content areas.

Transformed School System:

Students understand learning objectives and the criteria to be used in assessing their progress. They take pointers and encouragement from teachers to improve and meet expectations. Documentation in addition to test results—including project samples and individual and team reports recorded on compact discs and videotapes—is assembled in portfolios that provide evidence of student work and is carried forward through the years.

Individual standardized testing for all students is unnecessary. Standardized tests should be administered only to obtain results on samplings of students. Criterion-referenced assessment helps everyone meet specific learning objectives. Many kinds of documentation can record student achievement. These days, CDs and videotapes of student work can be sent to colleges, trade schools, or potential employers, and the parties can talk through interactive video to determine admission or hiring. Standardized test scores do not mean much in this context. Evidence of work is more meaningful.

Traditional School System:

Administrators rate teachers. Faculty rate students. Students rate themselves based on their grades. Students rate the staff based on the grades given.

Transformed School System:

Administrators, faculty, and students work together to enhance each other's learning and enjoyment of the learning process while improving instructional strategies.

Leaders are in the position to effect system change. Without leadership, we blame specific people for poor results. Blaming everyone must stop! Holding everyone accountable is a failure to understand the system. The system controls most of the decisions and procedures people use to achieve their tasks. The system generates 98 percent of the results of the system. We improve educational systems by educating, not blaming, the people within them. Teamwork is the key, not fault finding.

Traditional School System:

Instructional materials and supplies are procured at lowest cost.

Transformed School System:

The purchase of classroom materials is based on the quality of instruction they represent, their appropriateness for intended uses, and multiple theme application. Purchasing decisions are made on educational value, not cost alone.

Everything having to do with schools should be bought on a value-over-time basis, not on apparent initial cost savings. Poor quality in materials and workmanship, faulty decision-making processes, and poor purchasing decisions can be damaging to the system. As stewards of public funds, educators need to keep this in mind.

Traditional School System:

School officials at times pit suppliers against each other to gain low pricing.

Transformed School System:

Purchasing agents and others responsible for acquisition of equipment and supplies develop long-term relationships with businesses, always emphasizing value over time above cost over time.

Trust between school systems and the businesses that service them is essential. School customers get the most for their dollars, and the businesses can concentrate on providing quality products and service.

An equipment story illustrates this point. When I worked with Dr. Hitzmen, I was asked to present a proposal for new furniture for a new school. After visiting many schools and looking at the types of school furniture available, I knew what I wanted to recommend. However, my choices were somewhat costly, and the school board had a policy of taking the lowest bids on furniture. In my presentation to the board, I defined "lowest cost" as the initial expenditure plus five additional years of replacement or repair cost. Having requested information on furniture upkeep from the schools I had visited, I included this with my proposal. The more expensive furniture turned out to be less costly over the six-year period of use than any furniture whose list price was attractive at first glance. Board members saw the "value" of the expenditure, not the "cost" of the furniture, and approved the purchase of better-quality goods. More than twenty years later, most of the furniture acquired in that transaction is still in use.

Although children are not chairs, the principle is the same in an instructional context. The more that is invested in students in terms of sound curricular design and individual attention, the greater the yield for them, for teachers and administrators, for their families and the communities in which they live, and for society as a whole. In fact, it may seem an obvious point to make, but the potential return on energy and planning directed at young people is greater and far more significant than preservation of equipment and facilities.

Traditional School System:

Parents are largely excluded from instructional planning.

Transformed School System:

Parents are included in all planning phases to improve the process of instruction.

Parents are primary partners in the educational enterprise. They have a right to be involved, and their views are worthy of consideration.

Traditional School System:

Fads with little statistical evidence of their validity prompt instructional change.

Transformed School System:

Instructional innovation is based on conclusions drawn from analysis of carefully collected data.

Teachers need to be able to create and interpret control charts on student progress, and once they understand the difference between common and special causes for variation in achievement, they can provide special attention if required.

Traditional School System:

To survive and maintain cherished prerogatives, teachers in departments and grade levels work hard to protect their vested interests.

Transformed School System:

Everyone in the system is a partner with the aim of continually improving the educational system for everyone to win, everyone to gain.

A team effort is needed to achieve the common aim: creation of an environment that will sustain lifelong learning. There must be no losers in the system, because when anyone loses, everyone loses. Someone once told me a story that clearly makes this point. A married couple would argue constantly, he said, and one of the two would "win" the arguments most of the time. After observing the dynamics of these disputes for some time, a friend of the couple asked the person who always seemed to win, "How do you like being married to a loser?"

THE OPEN-ENDED FUTURE

Transformation is a race without a finish line, and those who enter it invest themselves in a lifelong commitment to improvement. Self-improvement and positive development in others lead to system-wide metamorphosis. The process requires knowledge and experience from the past and analysis of present realities. It calls for a new understanding of people.

Everywhere he went, W. Edwards Deming appealed to educators, industry leaders, and others in positions of influence, telling them he preferred "management by positive cooperation" over "management by conflict." He believed that people everywhere have the same need for respect and self-esteem. He recognized that changing any system involves commitment. He said time is of the essence. A man once approached Deming at a business conference and asked how he could change his company. Deming asked what the man was willing to do to change. The man said he would send all his people to Deming seminars. Deming asked again what he would do to change. The man insisted that he would have his people do anything. Deming persisted. "What will YOU do to change?" he asked. The man finally heard the question.

Do we hear this question? We surely need to, because profound change of lasting benefit begins with and within us. Look in a mirror. What you see is where it starts. If you are ready, read on!

REFERENCE

Deming, W.E. (1989). Speech in Osaka, Japan.

Confusing special and common causes are the greatest two mistakes. . . . Confusing common causes with special causes will only make things worse.

W. Edwards Deming

CHAPTER 5

SYSTEM VARIATION
UNDERSTANDING COMMON
AND SPECIAL CAUSES

My boyhood experience on a farm in Wisconsin taught me a lot. I learned about variation, for example, while tracking the milk production of our cows. We kept a record on each cow to monitor the volume of milk produced. Through that experience, I learned that such things as weather, amount of feed, and pasture conditions all had an impact on milk production. One thing was "for sure"—when the thermometer went up, milk production went down. We kept the records so we could determine which cows should be sold—because they didn't produce enough milk.

Another thing I learned was that the size of a cow wasn't related to the amount of milk she produced. Though small in size, my favorite cow, "Whitey," was one of our best producers. The reason I loved her so was that, as I would bring in the cows from the pasture for milking, she would walk behind me on the way to the barn and nudge me in the butt with her nose. She was so friendly my grandmother could walk up to her and milk her by hand in the field.

Although I experienced "common and special" causes of variation through my experience with milk production, I wasn't aware at that time of statistical control chart analysis. We understood low and high ranges and made decisions based on low numbers. Even though we probably made some wrong decisions about certain cows, I learned something about variation through that happy boyhood experience. I wish we would have known about control chart analysis. It would have helped us understand system average and dispersion more meaningfully, and we might have made better decisions.

Variation is the dispersion of values in a system. Dispersion is determined by the range, average, and standard deviation of the values in a system. The range is the difference between the highest and lowest values of the system, or within subsets of a system. The average is determined by adding the values of the system and dividing the resulting sum by the number of values in the system. The standard deviation is determined by the dispersion of values around the average of the system.

Understanding the dispersion of a system helps us analyze its variation. The clearer the picture of dispersion in a system, the better the capacity to improve the system—if that is needed. Improving a system is defined as moving the average of values toward the aim and reducing dispersion of values around the average. Both of these characteristics are necessary to achieve improvement.

As director of the Bell Telephone Laboratories in the early 1920s, Walter Shewhart studied variability, seeing that it determined both the need and the capacity for system improvement (Shewhart, 1986). In any system, there are a number of stages, steps, functions, and processes that introduce opportunities for variation beyond what is considered normal. Dr. Shewhart spoke of system variation in terms of its being in control, within limits, or out of control. He defined variation as "in control" if it is within specific limits and clearly a function of random variation of elements in a system. "Out of control" variation, he said, is outside specified limits and is caused by events not occurring randomly in the system.

These concepts are critical because they are the basis for continual improvement of any system. If variation in a system is in control, the system is predictable. If it is not in control, the system is unpredictable, and unpredictable systems are impossible to improve. Continual improvement depends on moving the average and reducing variation toward the aim. To improve a system, one must first bring it into control and then alter it to produce better results. Shewhart developed control charts to demonstrate these ideas. W. Edwards Deming gave Shewhart's work widespread exposure. The rest is history.

A reminder of some of the terms we have encountered thus far may be helpful here.

* A *system* is a group of related processes integrated to accomplish an aim.

* A *process* is a grouping of concurrent tasks directed at accomplishing one particular outcome.

* *Variation* within a system is the range and dispersion of individual events around the average in a process or number of processes.

* *Range* is the difference between the highest and lowest values in a system or subset of a system.

* *Dispersion* is the concentration of points around the system average.

* *Control limits* are statistical measures of the upper and lower limits within which variation of individual events ranges.

* *Statistical control* is a characteristic of a process in which variation is random and within upper and lower control limits.

* A *common cause* is a reason for random process variation that is predictable in the near future. A common cause leads to variation within the control limits.

* A *special cause* is a reason for process variation that is neither random nor predictable. It leads to variation outside the control limits.

* *Tampering* is acting on a common cause of variation as if it were a special cause and making the system worse.

A worker has no control over a process or system that is in statistical control. Improvement can occur in a stable system only if there is fundamental change. The strategy for improvement is first to stabilize all processes in the system at their "normal pattern of expectancy" and then involve willing workers, particularly those who know the process, to identify the complexities of each process step with the idea of improving or simplifying it.

Everyone has a role in process and system improvement. This is not something achieved simply by management desire. It requires knowledge. Managers must understand and take responsibility for improving the system by eliminating special causes and reducing common causes of variation within a process or system. Willing workers participate, but managers must first establish the proper environment, making it acceptable for people to identify problems that need to be solved. "Fire fighting"—that is, correcting mistakes—is critical but does not necessarily constitute improvement of the system. People need to be recognized for work that results in system improvement as well as for eliminating mistakes. Common causes of variation exist in any organization, and it is not good practice to deny them or try to cover them up. Over time, they will resurface, necessitating rework or extra work. For example, replacing a broken window is important to maintain internal heating, but it does not improve heat retention better than before the window was broken in the first place.

EXAMPLES OF VARIATION IN EDUCATIONAL SYSTEMS

A HABITUALLY LATE BUS DRIVER

In the school district in which I was a principal, the bus contract stated that buses were to arrive at buildings a half hour before class time. Classes began at 9 a.m. in our school, so buses were to be at the building at 8:30. I decided to record the arrival time of one of the buses, because it appeared the driver was consistently late. Over a one-month period involving twenty work days, I recorded the exact times when this bus arrived.

ARRIVAL TIMES

Day			Day		
	1	8:36		11	8:36
	2	8:37		12	8:31
	3	8:31		13	8:30
	4	8:35		14	8:50
	5	8:48		15	8:36
	6	8:33		16	8:32
	7	8:32		17	8:35
	8	8:35		18	8:32
	9	8:34		19	8:33
	10	8:30		20	8:34

Using these numbers, I determined the differences between each arrival time and the expected time of arrival.

ARRIVAL TIME DIFFERENCES

Day			
1 = 6	6 = 3	11 = 6	16 = 2
2 = 7	7 = 2	12 = 1	17 = 5
3 = 1	8 = 5	13 = 0	18 = 2
4 = 5	9 = 4	14 = 20	19 = 3
5 = 18	10 = 0	15 = 6	20 = 4

Then, using the following formula, I determined the mean ($\overline{X}$) of the variation.

$$\overline{X} = \text{MEAN} = \frac{\text{sum of time differences}}{\text{number of days}} = \frac{100}{20} = 5 \text{ minutes}$$
$$(N = 20)$$

Then I determined the "upper" and "lower" control limits of the variations and plotted the points on a graph.

upper/lower control limits = UCL = 5 + 6 = 11   UCL = 8:41
                             LCL = 5 - 6 = -1   LCL = 8:29

Plot the points on the graph shown in Figure 5.1:

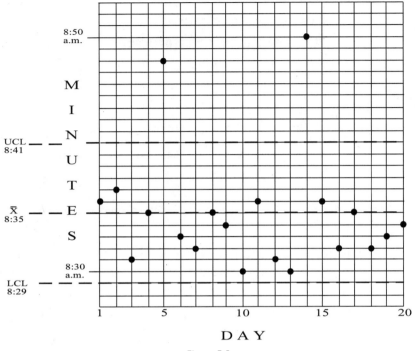

Figure 5.1
Variations Graph

A number of interesting issues came to light in this process. The average time of arrival by this driver was 8:35 a.m., five minutes after the contract time. Also, the arrival-time system was out of control based on the two points of 8:48 and 8:50 a.m. I called the driver in to talk about this. Observing the data I had collected, the driver explained that unavoidable family conditions had caused the extremely late arrivals on Days 5 and 14. I accepted this explanation and proceeded to look at the rest of the points as a stable "system in control" that was nonetheless unacceptable under the contract. When the driver could give no explanation for frequent lateness, I turned the discussion toward ways of improving the situation. We talked about several possible solutions, given the family obligations involved, and afterward the driver's arrival times improved.

STUDENT MISBEHAVIOR (LEONARD, 1992)

The administrator of a large middle school was concerned about student discipline. According to the discipline policy, three formal steps were to be taken in situations where rules of conduct were broken: written warnings to the student, with copies sent to his or her parents; detention after three written warnings; suspension for serious or repeated infractions. Listed in Figure 5.2 are the incidents requiring some kind of disciplinary action that took place in a twenty-week period. The administrator in this case:

- Plotted the data on a "c chart" (Wheeler and Chambers, 1992).

- Calculated the mean and the upper and lower control limits.

- Determined if the process was stable.

- Created an intervention to improve the process.

WEEK	INCIDENTS
1	8
2	13
3	7
4	11
5	9
6	15
7	10
8	9
9	20
10	13
11	11
12	10
13	8
14	13
15	5
16	9
17	11
18	10
19	6
20	10

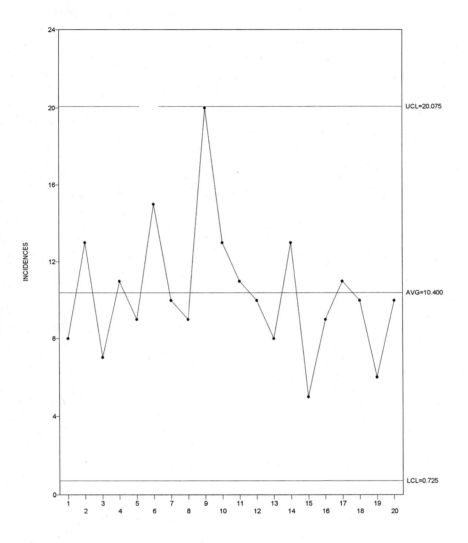

Figure 5.2
Control Chart: "Incidents" Recorded over One Semester

Any principal might have a tendency to overreact to the number of incidents in Week 9. However, the data indicate that student discipline is statistically in control—stable, in other words. It can be discouraging for a school staff to deal with a student body capable of generating up to twenty disciplinary incidents per week, but statistically the system is both "in control" and predictable. So it would be ill-advised to single out any event in any week as a special cause of variation. Intervention in response to any one week's experience would be tampering with the system. It could make the situation worse.

Because all twenty weeks of data are within the control limits, one can conclude that this is a stable system. No special causes are involved; all variation is due to common causes. If the results of this stable system are not acceptable, the system has to be improved to achieve better results. School administrators, teachers, and students must come up with solutions to the problem. If nothing is changed in the system, it will continue to produce the same results within a small range of variation.

DIFFERENCES IN STUDENT READING ABILITY

A middle school has five classes each in grades five through eight. State standardized tests are used each year to measure student reading achievement levels. Listed below, by grade level and class, are the number of students who tested under their grade level in reading. The administrator in this case took the following steps to improve the process.

- Plotted the data on a p chart (Wheeler and Chambers, 1992).

- Calculated the mean and the upper and lower control limits.

- Determined if the process is stable.

- Intervened to improve the process.

P Chart Analysis for Students Reading below Grade Level

Group	Grade Level	Class Size	Below Level	Proportion
1	5A	28	2	0.071
2	5B	27	3	0.111
3	5C	26	2	0.077
4	5D	28	5	0.179
5	5E	28	1	0.036
6	6A	29	2	0.069
7	6B	30	3	0.100
8	6C	29	4	0.138
9	6D	27	3	0.111
10	6E	26	1	0.038
11	7A	31	4	0.129
12	7B	27	6	0.222
13	7C	28	8	0.286
14	7D	29	5	0.172
15	7E	27	3	0.111
16	8A	30	1	0.033
17	8B	31	4	0.129
18	8C	28	3	0.107
19	8D	29	2	0.069
20	8E	27	5	0.185

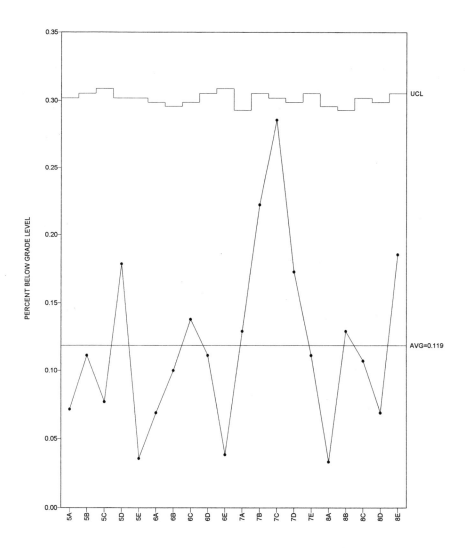

Figure 5.3
Students Reading below Grade Level

It would be inappropriate to bring in the teacher of Class 7C (Group 13) and suggest that poor teaching strategies are the root of the problem. The data indicate that this is a stable system. All variation is due to common causes. There are no special causes. Again, this does not mean the situation is acceptable. The reading instruction system must be changed, but no amount of complaining to teachers is going to make a difference. It could make things worse, because the system needs to be analyzed, new approaches should be taken, and the results studied. If new teaching methods lead to reading improvements, they can be incorporated into the system.

DIFFERENCES IN STUDENT AGES AT GRADE LEVELS

Even though the age ranges of the students seemed wide in each middle school grade level, each grade level was a stable system. I believe it is important to record the age range within grade levels to understand the normal variation within these levels. Many teachers and parents, and students as well, do not know how widely age varies. Understanding this helps explain the range of diversity and the need for designing instructional systems to meet this range. Grading and subsequent ranking of students has nothing to do with meeting instructional needs and helping students learn. Diversity in age and other factors, which accounts for most variation in learning, needs to be respected, not graded.

AGE VARIATION AT GRADE LEVELS

(Data taken from 1972-73 Grade Level Composition, Twin Groves School.)

Grade Level 5	9.10 9.12	10.0 10.2	10.3 10.5	10.6 10.8	10.9 10.11	10.12 11.1	11.2 11.4	11.5 11.7	11.8 11.10	11.11 12.0	12.1 12.3	12.4 12.6	12.7 12.9
# of Students	1	6	12	29	27	14	25	5	3	2	1	0	1

Grade Level 6	10.9 10.11	10.12 11.1	11.2 11.4	11.5 11.7	11.8 11.10	11.11 12.0	12.1 12.3	12.4 12.6	12.7 12.9	12.10 12.12
# of Students	0	0	2	12	22	18	34	16	5	4

Grade Level 7	11.5 11.7	11.8 11.10	11.11 12.0	12.1 12.3	12.4 12.6	12.7 12.9	12.10 12.12	13.0 13.2	13.3 13.5	13.6 13.8	13.9 13.11	13.12 14.1	14.2 14.4
# of Students	1	0	0	0	10	28	21	22	13	3	5	0	1

Grade Level 8	13.3 13.5	13.6 13.8	13.9 13.11	13.12 14.1	14.2 14.4	14.5 14.7	14.8 14.10	14.11 15.0	15.1 15.3	15.4 15.6	15.7 15.9
# of Students	6	24	13	19	22	4	4	1	0	0	1

Figure 5.4
All Children at a Given Grade Level Are the Same Age

The following data analysis shows that each grade level is in statistical control. Each grade demonstrates normal variation.

Average Age (mo)	f	(mo)f
119	1	119
121	6	726
124	12	1488
127	29	3683
130	27	3510
133	14	1862
135	25	3375
138	5	690
141	3	423
144	2	288
146	1	146
149	0	0
152	1	152
TOTALS	126	16462

$$\overline{X} = \frac{(mo)f}{f} = \frac{16462}{126} = 130.7$$

$$R = 33 \text{ months}$$

$$UCL/LCL = \overline{X} \pm 3\sqrt{\overline{X}}$$
$$= 130.7 \pm 3(11.4)$$
$$= 130.7 \pm 34.4$$

$$UCL = 130.7 + 34.3 = 165.0 \text{ months}$$
$$LCL = 130.7 - 34.3 = 96.4 \text{ months}$$

Figure 5.5
Grade 5

Average Age (mo)	f	(mo)f
138	1	138
141	0	0
144	0	0
146	0	0
149	10	1490
152	28	4256
155	21	3255
157	22	3454
160	13	2080
163	3	489
166	5	830
168	0	0
171	1	171
TOTALS	104	16163

$$\overline{X} = \frac{(mo)f}{f} = \frac{16163}{104} = 155.4$$

$$R = 33 \text{ months}$$

$$UCL/LCL = \overline{X} \pm 3\sqrt{\overline{X}}$$
$$= 155.4 \pm 37.4$$

$$UCL = 155.4 + 37.4 = 192.8 \text{ months}$$
$$LCL = 155.4 - 37.4 = 118.0 \text{ months}$$

Figure 5.6
Grade 6

$$\overline{X} = \frac{(mo)f}{f} = \frac{16348}{113} = 144.7$$

Average Age (mo)	f	(mo)f
135	2	270
138	12	1656
141	22	3102
144	18	2592
146	34	4964
149	16	2384
152	5	760
155	4	620
TOTALS	113	16348

R = 20 months

$$UCL/LCL = \overline{X} \pm 3\sqrt{\overline{X}}$$
$$= 144.7 \pm 3(12)$$
$$= 144.7 \pm 36$$

UCL = 144.7 + 36 = 180.7 months
LCL = 144.7 - 36 = 108.7 months

Figure 5.7
Grade 7

Average Age (mo)	f	(mo)f
160	6	960
163	24	3912
166	13	2158
168	19	3192
171	22	3762
174	4	696
177	4	708
180	1	180
182	0	0
185	0	0
188	1	188
TOTALS	94	15756

$$\overline{X} = \frac{(mo)f}{f} = \frac{15756}{94} = 167.6$$

R = 28 months

$$UCL/LCL = \overline{X} \pm 3\sqrt{\overline{X}}$$
$$= 167.6 \pm 38.8$$

UCL = 167.6 + 38.8 = 206.4 months
LCL = 167.6 - 38.8 = 128.8 months

Figure 5.8
Grade 8

READING LEVELS ASSESSED AT GRADE LEVEL

Everyone at a given grade within a traditional school setting is expected to achieve at the same level. Let us study the data from an assessment test in reading:

Grade Level	Grade Level Equivalent										Total
	3	4	5	6	7	8	9	10	11	12	
5	4	11	22	31	28	15	7	8			126
6	1	2	11	26	21	15	18	11	7	4	116
7	2	1		15	11	24	13	12	16	11	105
8		2	3	3	11	16	17	13	8	21	94
Total At Each Level	7	16	36	75	71	70	55	44	31	36	441

Figure 5.9
A Reading Assessment Test

The idea that children at the same grade level achieve at the same level is totally inaccurate. The data in Figure 5.9 should make this clear.

Figures 5.10 and 5.11 provide an analysis of the data in Figure 5.9:

Average Age (GL)	f	(GL)f
3	4	12
4	11	44
5	22	110
6	31	186
7	28	196
8	15	120
9	7	63
10	8	80
11	0	0
12	0	0
TOTALS	126	811

$$\overline{GL} = \frac{118}{126} = 6.4$$

$$\begin{aligned} UCL/LCL &= \overline{GL} \pm 3\sqrt{\overline{GL}} \\ &= 6.4 \pm 3\sqrt{6.4} \\ &= 6.4 \pm 7.6 \end{aligned}$$

$$UCL = 6.4 + 7.6 = 14 \text{ (Grade Level)}$$
$$LCL = 6.4 - 7.6 = 0 \text{ (Grade Level)}$$

Figure 5.10
Grade 5

Average Age (GL)	f	(GL)f
3	1	3
4	2	8
5	11	55
6	26	156
7	21	147
8	15	120
9	18	162
10	11	110
11	7	77
12	4	48
TOTALS	116	886

$$\overline{GL} = \frac{886}{116} = 7.6$$

$$UCL/LCL = \overline{GL} \pm 3\sqrt{\overline{GL}}$$
$$= 7.6 \pm 3\sqrt{7.6}$$
$$= 7.6 \pm 8.3$$

$$UCL = 7.6 + 8.3 = 15.9 \text{ (Grade Level)}$$
$$LCL = 7.6 - 8.3 = 0 \quad \text{(Grade Level)}$$

Figure 5.11
Grade 6

Average Age (GL)	f	(GL)f
3	2	6
4	1	4
5	0	0
6	15	90
7	11	77
8	24	192
9	13	117
10	12	120
11	16	176
12	11	132
TOTALS	105	914

$$\overline{GL} = \frac{914}{105} = 8.7$$

$$UCL/LCL = \overline{GL} \pm 3\sqrt{\overline{GL}}$$
$$= 8.7 \pm 3\sqrt{8.7}$$
$$= 8.7 \pm 8.8$$

$$UCL = 8.7 + 8.8 = 17.5 \text{ (Grade Level)}$$
$$LCL = 8.7 - 8.8 = 0 \quad \text{(Grade Level)}$$

Figure 5.12
Grade 7

Average Age (GL)	f	(GL)f
4	2	8
5	3	15
6	3	18
7	11	77
8	16	128
9	17	153
10	13	130
11	8	88
12	21	252
TOTALS	94	869

$$\overline{GL} = \frac{869}{94} = 9.2$$

$$UCL/LCL = \overline{GL} \pm 3\sqrt{\overline{GL}}$$
$$= 9.2 \pm 3\sqrt{9.2}$$
$$= 9.2 \pm 9.1$$

$$UCL = 9.2 + 9.1 = 18.3 \text{ (Grade Level)}$$
$$LCL = 9.2 - 9.1 = .1 \quad \text{(Grade Level)}$$

Figure 5.13
Grade 8

Consider all fifth-grade children between the ages of 11.2 through 11.4 in the area of reading:

Fifth-Grade Reading Results
Ages 11 Years, 2 Months through 11 Years, 4 Months

Grade Level Equivalency	3	4	5	6	7	8	9	(7 levels)
Number of Students	1	3	8	3	2	3	5	(25)

To assume that just because children are the same age they will achieve at the same level is a gross misunderstanding of reality. Yet this is the common understanding of many people, and it dictates expectations of their children and of the school their children attend. Little thought is given to individual differences and the different rates of learning of each child.

The statistical analysis of these data in Figure 5.14 is necessary to understand this system.

$$\overline{GL} = \frac{156}{25} = 6.2$$

Average Age (GL)	f	(GL)f
3	1	3
4	3	12
5	8	40
6	3	18
7	2	14
8	3	24
9	5	45
TOTALS	25	156

$$UCL/LCL = \overline{GL} \pm 3\sqrt{\overline{GL}}$$
$$= 6.2 \pm 3\sqrt{6.2}$$
$$= 6.2 \pm 7.5$$

$$UCL = 6.2 + 7.5 = 13.7$$
$$LCL = 6.2 - 7.5 = 0$$

Figure 5.14
Same-Age Students (11.2–11.4)

The range of reading scores is stable at each of the grade levels. All the grade-level data fall within the upper and lower control limits. All this variation is random. I believe this range in scores is typical of most middle school students and would not be surprising to educators. However, I believe most parents and most people would find it surprising that this is normal variation. Also, the variation in the performance of children of ages 11 years and 2 months through 11 years and 4 months is stable. Here again, I think most people would not expect so much reading-level variation in children the same age. Some might think something is wrong with the reading program. In this school, parent conferences take place each semester, yet many parents miss their appointments.

Semester	Appointments Missed	Appointments Scheduled
Fall 88	51	200
Spring 89	32	200
Fall 89	19	200
Spring 90	60	200
Fall 90	45	200
Spring 91	70	200
Fall 91	53	200
Spring 92	42	200
Fall 92	63	200
Spring 93	57	200

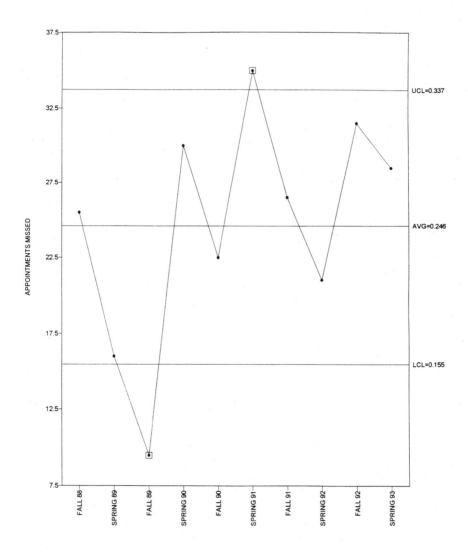

Figure 5.15
P Chart for Parent-Teacher Conferences

In Figure 5.15, we can see that two points are out of control: the fall semester of 1989 and the spring semester of 1991. Each situation must be investigated to understand why there is so much variation, and, after the investigation is made, something must be done to remove negative effects from the system and bring it into control. It happens that the fall of 1989 point is out of control in a positive direction—fewer missed appointments. Whatever led to this fortunate situation should be built into the system, if possible, to foster good attendance. Spring 1991 is out of control in a negative way, however. Whatever caused so many parents to miss appointments in that semester should be eliminated from the system if possible. Each of these analyses is important in understanding the special causes of variation and helping to improve the system in the future.

IMPLICATIONS FOR EDUCATORS

- It is important to know the difference between common causes of variation in a system and special causes attributable to outside causes.

- Special causes of variation should be thoroughly examined to find out how and why they exist.

- Avoid Mistake #1: Treating a common cause of variation of any kind as a special cause. This is known as "tampering" with a system, and it usually makes a situation worse.

- Avoid Mistake #2: Treating a special cause of variation as a common cause and not investigating it with all due speed, allowing the system to remain unstable, not in control, and not predictable.

- To bring an unstable system into a control state, one needs to remove special causes of variation.

- Work on improving the system once special causes have been explained and eliminated.

- Improve the average (mean) and reduce variation around the mean to improve the system.

- Continually clarify the system aim.

- Value people in the system.

- Demonstrate system improvement statistically.

- Change from outside is needed to improve the system.

DETRIMENTAL COMMON-CAUSE VARIATIONS

- Teachers teaching teachers in new instructional programs

- A single teacher making changes in instructional strategies or curricular selections without peer review

- A school faculty making curricular changes without community input

- Any attempt to change a system by responding to a single case

Variations of this kind hurt a system because the people responsible for them do not understand how the system works. They act independently, hoping to advance a single concern and showing little respect for the integrity of other people or the system.

DETRIMENTAL SPECIAL-CAUSE VARIATIONS

- Anyone intentionally not following procedure

- Anyone failing to accept appropriately delegated responsibilities

- Anyone withholding needed information from someone who must make a decision on available data

- Anyone intentionally compromising the system

- Anyone engaging in win-lose negotiating

While these special causes are bothersome in various ways, the common theme is that those responsible appear to care only about personal gain.

REFERENCES

Leonard, J.F. (1992). *Essential statistical methods for total quality schools.* 79 Cady Lane, Woodstock, CT 06281.

Shewhart, W. (1986). *Statistical method from the viewpoint of quality control.* New York: Dover Publications.

Wheeler, D.J., and Chambers, D.S. (1992). *Understanding statistical process control* (2d ed.). Knoxville, TN: SPC Press, pp. 273-74, 263-70.

The system of profound knowledge provides a lens. It provides a new map of theory by which to understand and optimize the organizations that we work in, and thus to make a contribution to the whole country.

W. Edwards Deming

CHAPTER 6

KNOWLEDGE
PREDICTION THAT LEADS TO IMPROVEMENT

I have a friend who was always late to meetings. The average time late was about thirty minutes—a stable system. Since I was planning an important event and wanted to be sure my friend would be on time, I decided to apply Dr. Deming's maxim that "knowledge" is the ability to predict future behavior, based on past events, within the context of testing a theory. Here is how it went:

Theory: My friend is usually thirty minutes late for meetings.

Practice: State the starting time for the event to my friend as thirty minutes earlier than the actual starting time.

Prediction: My friend will be on time for the event.

Result: My friend was on time and I was relieved.

Dr. Walter Shewhart's work reminds us that data provide us with measurements. However, a measure is only as good as the measurement strategy used at that time. Change the measurement strategy, and you get a different number. Theory must be the basis of all investigation, and thoroughly tested theory must be the basis for any action taken to improve any system.

COMPONENTS OF KNOWLEDGE

Knowledge is the analysis and interpretation of data that leads to prediction. Prediction is based on theory, and hopefully it will be verified by the performance of the system. Another way of saying this is to declare that knowledge is the ability to predict system behavior for the purpose of system improvement.

The three components of knowledge are:

- data of *experience* in which the process of "knowing" begins (E)

- degree of *belief* (Pb) in the *prediction* based on the original data or some summary thereof as *evidence* (E)

- *prediction* in terms of data that one would expect to get if certain experiments were to be performed in the future (P)

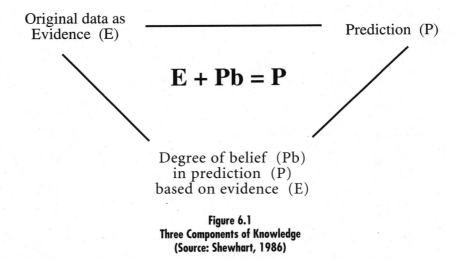

$$E + Pb = P$$

Original data as Evidence (E)

Prediction (P)

Degree of belief (Pb)
in prediction (P)
based on evidence (E)

Figure 6.1
Three Components of Knowledge
(Source: Shewhart, 1986)

Evidence consists of understanding the results of the present system. This understanding is based on current data from the process as it is actually functioning. The degree of belief in prediction of the system is based on statistical analysis of current evidence. This analysis provides a picture of the range, average, and standard deviation from the average of the current system as it is performing with respect to factors or results being considered. Also, an understanding of common and special causes

94

in the evidence is critical. Prediction, therefore, is based on the evidence and the degree of confidence one has in analysis of it. All of this enables us to have knowledge—understanding of the present system to the extent of being able to predict its performance.

If the original data are stable—in control—the system generating the data is highly predictable in the near future. Knowing this enables us to develop a theory that forecasts system performance. If the results are desirable, the system should be kept in that state, of course. If the results are unacceptable, intervention strategies should be introduced and the results studied to determine if any improvement has been made. If the original data are not stable—not in control—special causes of deviation from what is expected must be identified and removed from the situation. Unless the data are brought into control, no predictability is possible. If the behavior of the system is unpredictable, no amount of intervention for improvement can be understood. To be effective, work on the system should proceed according to the following pattern:

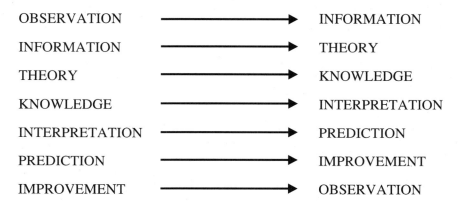

OBSERVATION	$\longrightarrow$	INFORMATION
INFORMATION	$\longrightarrow$	THEORY
THEORY	$\longrightarrow$	KNOWLEDGE
KNOWLEDGE	$\longrightarrow$	INTERPRETATION
INTERPRETATION	$\longrightarrow$	PREDICTION
PREDICTION	$\longrightarrow$	IMPROVEMENT
IMPROVEMENT	$\longrightarrow$	OBSERVATION

Figure 6.2
Logical Sequences for Improvement

In late 1988, the Illinois legislature voted to create local school councils, or boards of education, for each school in Chicago. It was thought that this would improve education. In the years since this action was taken, Chicago schools have not improved. The legislative action was based on the theory that governance at the school level would increase learning. From the outset, one might have questioned the supposed relationship between local governance and academic achievement. What evidence is there of this relationship? Was this theory tested elsewhere before it was introduced in Chicago? If we do not know the theory that is being tested by the system we are observing, we risk not learning anything about the system. Collecting data is a meaningless exercise unless it increases our knowledge of what the system is doing or might be capable of doing. Theory is what helps us understand how to improve a system.

Also, existing theory needs to be tested against new data, and unless information is interpreted in a theoretical framework, it is only information, not knowledge.

EXAMPLE:

Theory: Local school governance will increase learning.

Acting on this theory:

Create local governance ➡	Better academic achievement
In place one year ➡	No difference in academic achievement
In place second year ➡	No difference in academic achievement

Conclusion: Local school governance may not be related to academic achievement.

OPERATIONAL DEFINITIONS

There is no such thing as a fact concerning an empirical observation or an observable experience. Two people seeing something at the same time may see it differently. Also, two people having the same experience at the same time may differ as to what is important in it. The aim of the system must be operationally defined by those who work in it. To assess the degree of improvement in a system, all participants must agree to the operationally defined aim and on methods to gather and analyze data. Terms such as academic expectations, achievement, improvement, learning, value added, meeting expectations, and many others must be understood by everyone. Along with these definitions, examples are helpful to clarify understanding of the meaning.

THEORY OF KNOWLEDGE APPLIED TO EDUCATION

To understand the theory of knowledge in an academic setting, consider with me the idea of *inclusion*. Immediately, an operational definition is needed for the term. I am not suggesting that everyone agree with this definition, but for the purposes of discussion let us say that if any student who meets entry-level academic requirements for a course is welcome to enroll in it, the situation illustrates the principle of inclusion. Based on this definition, any other limitations students have would not keep them out of the course unless they couldn't meet entry-level academic requirements as well. What theory about the situation does this definition put forward? Students with various limitations (physical, emotional, or neurological) can learn in regular classrooms. A corollary to this is that all students can succeed. Another word needs an operational definition here, however. To *succeed* is to meet agreed-upon expectations in each student's academic improvement plan. (Note, "each student's plan.")

Now this theory needs to be tested. Data need to be gathered and interpreted, conclusions drawn, and recommendations stated. There is a lot of information on academic achievement of students with a full range of "normal" to "limited" abilities in areas of physical, emotional, and neurological difficulties. To go forward from here, however, we need other definitions. "Normal behavior" is that which is within statistically normal distribution patterns. It does not necessarily mean desirable. Statistical normality means the behavior occurs randomly within the common distribution of the population being studied. "Limited" means that to function at an entry level of the academic class in question, the student needs support from another. As suggested earlier, there is a great deal of assessment data on the academic achievement of students with disabilities. According to the inclusion hypothesis, the achievement of other students will not be negatively affected by including students with special limitations in regular classrooms. In fact, such a policy may lead to increased achievement overall. Everyone has limitations, and it is good to learn to work with people regardless of what those are.

Much planning would be necessary to test this theory. Classes would be selected for study, students assigned, support systems set up for special-needs students, and teachers trained to meet the student needs. Once academic interventions have been implemented over a prescribed period of time, additional assessment would be required. Conclusions could then be drawn and recommendations made. Data would be collected in at least the following areas: academic performance, understanding human limitations, and attitudes about working with others in class. Based on the analysis of this information, new knowledge would be obtained, and this would lead to acceptance, modification, or rejection of the inclusion theory. If the society values inclusion as a concept, continual improvement of strategies for implementing it would be the challenge at hand.

Dr. Deming suggested that a theory be tested first on a trial basis and in a limited way so as not to worsen a situation if the theory is unworkable or not a good idea. Much can be learned from this caution. Fads and bandwagon implementation of various ideas might be prevented if more educators took this to heart.

Many of us are impressed by people who have a lot of experience in particular areas. It is common to equate experience with knowledge. The fact is that experience teaches us nothing if it is not framed in the testing of a theory. Years of experience may teach a person only to continue with what is familiar, even if it is not the best way. This applies to specialists of all kinds—house painters, car mechanics, plumbers, physicians, teachers, or building contractors. New theories have been tested and new and better practices developed, yet people in these professions hang on to present and past ways of doing things. What if experience is negative or contains wrong information or destructive teachings? Clinging to these methods could sub-optimize an entire system. Experience is valuable, but it needs to be integrated with theory to create knowledge—the ability to predict for system improvement.

One reason grading students is meaningless and destructive is that grades cannot be used for predicting the future contributions of any person. The grade is a number based on objective and subjective evaluation. It may have little validity for the future. Many of us, if we believed in the grades *we* were given, would not be where we are today; we would have given up on ourselves, quit, and not made the contributions we have to our families and society.

We know people learn in different ways and at different rates. We need to respect these differences and help each person learn through different instructional designs. The more we understand the people with whom we work, and the more we understand our students, the more sensitive we can be to what meets learning needs and preferences. Preferences are to be valued, not discriminated against. This is all part of valuing people and understanding diversity.

REFERENCES

Shewhart, W. (1986). *Statistical method from the viewpoint of quality control*. New York: Dover Publications, pp. 85-86.

One is born with intrinsic motivation, self-esteem, dignity, cooperation, curiosity, joy in learning. These attributes are high at the beginning of life, but are gradually crushed by the forces of destruction.

W. Edwards Deming

CHAPTER 7

HUMAN PSYCHOLOGY
Enhancing Intrinsic Motivation

I'll never forget the note my mother handed to me when I was old enough to understand what "adoption" meant:

> Not Flesh of My Flesh
> Not Bone of My Bone
> But Still Miraculously My Own
> Never Forget for a Single Minute
> You Did Not Grow Under My Heart but In It.

> *(Anonymous)*

This is why I am who I am today. I was blessed with a mother who accepted me as her son, unconditionally. I never looked back. I had no reason to!

We are all born with self-esteem, curiosity, and the desire to learn. Early in life, we are shaped by our parents and relatives as to how we are valued, loved, cared for, and taught. Unfortunately, the early years of life are not positive for many children. Abuse, neglect, drug addiction from birth, and other destructive trends seem to be on the rise in our country. Wherever the home environment is loving and supportive, however, children have early years that are for the most part joyous, and their learning is self-motivated and amazing. I believe this is still the case for the vast majority of children. Thus, in the beginning, most children come to school with enthusiasm and interest that would please any teacher. In fact, in the first few years of their experience in the system, children like school and enjoy learning. Few want to miss the opportunity to be with friends and make discoveries. They willingly help each other.

Within a few years, however, traditional indicators of teacher encouragement for the primary grades (smiley faces, gold stars, and the like) are replaced with letter grades and numerical scores. This change usually begins to take place around third grade. Numbers or grades become the primary means by which teachers communicate their responses to student effort and achievement. As years go on, a student's personal value tends to be equated with the grades, standardized test scores, and grade-point averages. Also, as they advance through the K-12 system, some students are grouped into smaller classes and given labels. Others are given privileges and attend events that are not open to all. Lists of the "best" students are posted, and others are made to feel of less value. Everyone talks about grades. Few discuss learning. Students leave high school understanding that the score, the grade, the average is the name of the game. The message is clear: getting results is all that counts.

The world of work reinforces this extrinsic reward system through management systems based on objectives and the bottom line of profit or loss. Other strategies such as incentive pay come into play. Again and again, people learn that the result, not the process, is what matters. In addition, as people advance in the work realm, they learn that they must compete to get ahead. Some day, perhaps, they will achieve the corner office with windows—standard proof of organizational success. Much game playing and manipulation takes place in getting to the top, or almost to the top. Somewhere along the line, most of us usually ask ourselves what this is all about. What is the point in this tooth-and-claw quest for success? Is money an adequate reward for the effort and heartache involved? What became of the idea of taking pleasure in work and work relationships? Where is the notion of justifiable pride in creating a product or service of value? Then it dawns on us that we have been cheated, lied to, and devalued. In one way or another, all have been dealt a bad hand. In large measure, school and work systems have eliminated natural joy in learning, personal motivation, and self-esteem, as well as in people's willingness to cooperate with each other.

There is much evidence that extrinsic reward systems do not satisfy people's real needs. Deep and long-lasting satisfaction, rather, comes from completion of meaningful tasks, recognition for a job of work well done, and being given personal responsibility and opportunities to advance. It should be noted that all these sources of fulfillment have to do with work processes. Generally speaking, people are not lazy. They want to work and want work to be pleasurable. They want to take pride in what they produce. They want opportunities to cooperate with others. And, of course, they want to be able to pay their bills. In most instances, what people dislike about their work experience has to do with personal relations in the workplace and working conditions, not the work itself. Levels of administration and evaluation systems create unrest between and among employees. In an atmosphere of competition for position, power, and control, everyone suffers, and the system is hobbled in its effectiveness.

Many people believe money is a positive motivator. In other words, if people are paid more, the system or situation will improve—or so it is said. Wrong! Wages and salaries are unrelated to system quality. In the context of education, teacher pay could be doubled, and the quality of the instructional program would not increase. Quality is determined by the methods used to achieve it, not by extrinsic reward, no matter how attractive that might be. Most teachers have no method for assessing the quality of the instructional process. Most do not see the importance of understanding the educational system as a whole, clarifying the aim and gathering data for the sake of improving the learning process. Many don't know how to analyze their work effectiveness.

Extrinsic motivational systems lead people to rule over others, protect what they have, avoid punishment, compete with rather than co-operate with co-workers, exaggerate their importance to make personal gains, misuse money, and maintain a mediocre status quo. Only intrinsically motivated people will want to improve the system in which they are working. System optimization and personal fulfillment are best achieved in an atmosphere of mutual respect and cooperation. Organizational leaders are responsible for creating such an atmosphere. To do this, they need to work on faulty processes, not judge the people whose work is hampered by those processes. Leaders must continually make this distinction, realizing that when people are understood and appreciated, they feel valued, and when they feel valued, they are productive. Leaders are responsible for creating the proper environment for people to achieve system aims.

Figure 7.1 lists the types of behavior that destroy self-esteem, dignity, and pride.

OPTIMIZATION:

Born with a desire to learn, self-esteem, curiosity, intrinsic motivation and dignity.

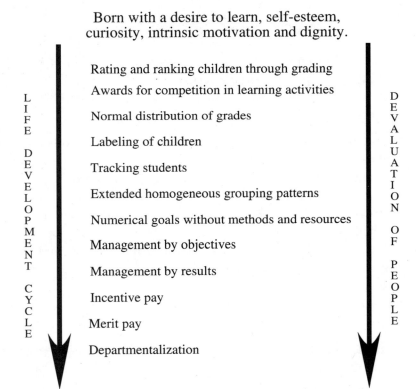

LIFE DEVELOPMENT CYCLE

Rating and ranking children through grading

Awards for competition in learning activities

Normal distribution of grades

Labeling of children

Tracking students

Extended homogeneous grouping patterns

Numerical goals without methods and resources

Management by objectives

Management by results

Incentive pay

Merit pay

Departmentalization

DEVALUATION OF PEOPLE

SUBOPTIMIZATION:

Kills joy in learning, self-esteem, intrinsic motivation, cooperation with others and self-worth.

Figure 7.1
Devaluation Behavior

p a r t

3

The
Right
Turn

There is no substitute for knowledge. Hard work, best efforts, and best intentions will not by themselves produce quality. Transformation of management is required.

W. Edwards Deming

CHAPTER 8

CONTINUAL IMPROVEMENT
CONCEPTS AND IMPLICATIONS

Dr. Deming often said, "Experience alone teaches nothing." Without theory, experience yields information rather than knowledge—opinion rather than wisdom. The most valuable kind of knowledge is that which provides a basis for prediction leading to system improvement, and numbers are a useful tool in acquiring such knowledge. As I have said in several ways up to this point, individual test scores are not to be equated with personal worth or ability, and aggregate test scores are not the only measure of a school or school system's success. Scholastic test-data analysis is nonetheless an important part of educational leadership. It is impossible to know where to begin improving an instructional system without knowing the levels of performance that are typical of young learners at different ages. In this light, a basic element of statistics, the concept of "normal distribution," provides a clue to prediction.

WHAT IS NORMAL?

Webster's dictionary defines "normal" as a pattern typical in the behavior of a social group. The normal distribution of performance in a system is pictured in Figure 8.1.

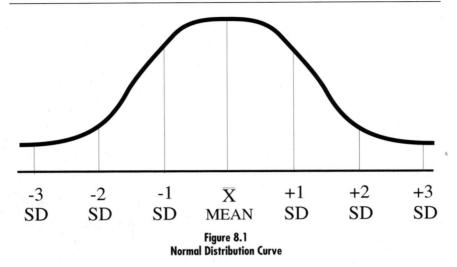

Figure 8.1
Normal Distribution Curve

±1 Standard Deviation means 68 percent of the population is dispersed within this measure.

±2 Standard Deviations means 95 percent of the population is dispersed within this measure.

±3 Standard Deviations means 99 percent of the population is dispersed within this measure.

A standard-deviation measure includes the area under the curve in both directions, plus and minus, from the mean (average) of the distribution being studied. Shewhart and Deming interpret ±3 standard deviations from the mean to be representative of 100 percent of the system being studied.

Any system generates results that cluster randomly around a mean (average), or ($\overline{X}$) value. For example, if we were to give a reading test to 100 fifth graders in a single school, we would expect their performance to reflect a "fifth-grade mean value." In other words, 68 percent of their scores would fall within 1 standard deviation from the mean, 95 percent of the scores would be within 2 standard deviations of the mean, and 100 percent of the scores would be within 3 standard deviations of the mean. This pattern is considered normal. Every student would not be performing at the mean value, and the variance from that point would be random and dispersed throughout the ±3 standard-deviation range.

Generally speaking, however, educators have misapplied this principle. One way they have done this is by trying to establish "tolerances" for letter grades, as in the idea that the "A range" for student performances on tests will be 95 to 100 percent. (See Figure 8.2.) This distorts the meaning of normal distribution, for no matter what group one assesses, the distribution within the group will follow a pattern, and that may or may not match teacher expectations. The inclination to set grade limitations comes from the mistaken notion that specification limits can be set without understanding random variation of the system. Also, expectations may be set without understanding normal distribution of the task for a defined population.

Another example of misperception in education is what happens when a school population increases its overall reading-level achievement by six months. Individual students may remain in the same position in the test score distribution (see A and B in Figure 8.2), so it could appear that they have not improved when in fact they have, and misleading judgments about individual student capabilities can be damaging. Rating and ranking of students and schools as a whole can go on for years with those in charge not understanding how to improve the system—or perhaps not seeing any need for improvement. Notice the comparison of numerical scores in Figure 8.2.

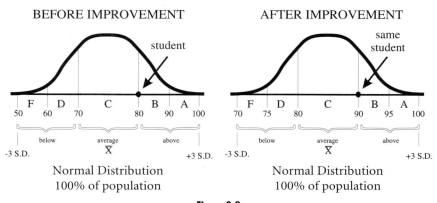

Figure 8.2
Reading Scores Distribution

The entire system improves, yet this improvement is not evident using the Specification Limits Model as pictured in the above figures.

STATISTICAL CONTROL

If student-performance data reflect normal distribution as just described, a situation is said to be "in control." Generally, if the performance of a system has its data points randomly distributed, there is no set pattern, and if the distribution meets the percentage limits specified, the system is said to be "in statistical control." It may be producing unacceptable results, but we can't hope to improve it unless it is in this stable state. If a system is unpredictable, we don't know that any attempt to improve it will be effective, and no firm conclusion can be drawn from any intervention tried.

The people observing the data must decide if the system is performing well based on the system aim. If the people agree that the system is doing what they want it to do, they should leave it alone and continue to monitor it.

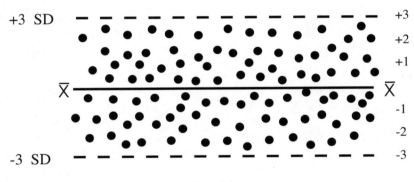

Figure 8.3
System in Statistical Control

The system will yield the same results time after time forever, within a small margin of variation. However, if the system is not generating desirable results, it needs to be studied and new approaches taken.

GETTING THE PICTURE

Walter Shewhart is known for developing control charts. These pictorial representations help those studying a system to distinguish between performance variations of two kinds: those that are systemic (the result of common causes within the system) and those that are assignable to special causes. Special variations can usually be detected by an expert on the job and removed from the system. A process is in statistical control when it is no longer afflicted with special causes of variation. A process in statistical control is predictable. According to the rule established by Shewhart for structuring control charts, we can be relatively sure that 100 percent of a large set of future observations under a defined method will have an average ($\overline{X}$) and dispersion of observations around that average of ±3 standard deviation (Shewhart, 1986).

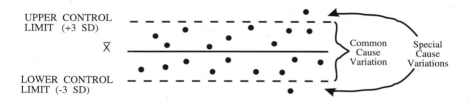

Figure 8.4
Control Chart

The same level of system variation will continue forever unless some change is introduced. If the reading performance of the fifth-grade students is in statistical control, the variation in test scores can be accounted for by considering differences in student background, student capacity, instructional materials, teaching strategies, classroom facilities, home environment, individual learning styles, and other factors that contribute to random variation. Other variations may stem from external forces or events. Some reading scores may fall outside the normal pattern because of learning disabilities, lack of training, test errors, and other reasons. Unusual cases must be investigated and understood in order to bring the system into control. If $\overline{X}$ ±3 SD is considered the normal distribution and accepted as such, performance that falls below the -3 SD level must be considered "special" and should be addressed differently. Special efforts must be made to bring performance into the normal range ($\overline{X}$ ±3 SD). If performance occurs above the +3 SD level, the positive reasons should be assessed and created for all to benefit if possible. In this way, the entire system can improve for all to gain.

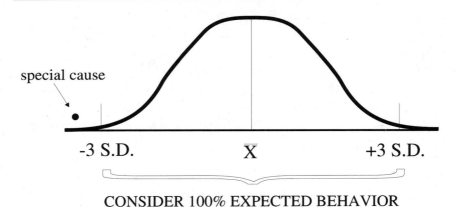

special cause

-3 S.D. $\overline{X}$ +3 S.D.

CONSIDER 100% EXPECTED BEHAVIOR

Figure 8.5
Special Cause to Be Investigated

Loss Function

Why might parents and teachers be concerned if a student has a reading score of 70 percent instead of 80 percent? The concept of "loss function," first developed in 1960 by Genichi Taguchi, provides an explanation (Taguchi, 1981). Dr. Taguchi's idea is that the greater the amount of variation from the desired result, the greater the loss to the organizational aim and society. This concept defines "World Class Quality" as performance that is "On Target with Minimum Variance." Educators have initiated a number of such management trends, including "zero defects," conforming to "specification limits" or "six sigma (+6 SD) specifications," "outcome-based objectives," and benchmarking. Yet all such approaches to setting higher standards miss the point of continual improvement. "World Class Quality" has been defined by or equated with "On Target with Minimum Variance" for the past thirty years, according to Wheeler and Chambers (1992).

The loss function idea includes the issue of desirability versus acceptability. In elementary education, for example, it is perfectly acceptable for students at certain stages to know how to spell words correctly in often-confused groupings like "to, two, and too" or "whether and weather" only on spelling tests. Students who can spell such words when they hear them pronounced, however, may not be able to spell them correctly in a sentence context. Appropriate use of these words in the natural

112

course of written expression is proof of high-level learning—and is actually the desired aim. In other words, while hitting a target in archery might be "acceptable," hitting the bull's-eye is certainly "desirable." Continual improvement creates ever higher standards.

ACCEPTABLE   DESIRABLE

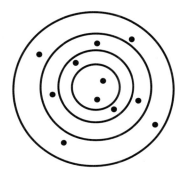   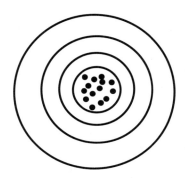

Figure 8.6
Acceptability vs. Desirability

As higher standards are created, they become the standards for future performance. Simply setting standards does not address the improvement process, and setting standards without a method of improving system processes may actually worsen the situation under study. The use of arbitrary standards with no method of analyzing the process may lead people to cheat to produce the expected results.

Here is another example of the loss function effect. If the temperature in a room is 72 degrees, almost everyone in it will be comfortable. If the temperature drops to 68 degrees, some people will be uncomfortable. If the temperature drops to 64 degrees, more people will become uncomfortable. If the thermometer reading drops to 60 degrees, almost everyone in the room will be uncomfortable. According to loss function theory, even though the temperature drops by equal increments (4 degrees each time), the effect of the amounts is not the same. Rather, it grows dramatically. The same would hold true in this example if the temperatures went up by 4-degree increments. People's reactions would be noticeably more intense with each change. The following figure illustrates this phenomenon.

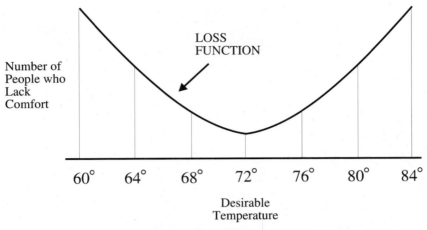

Number of
People who
Lack
Comfort

LOSS
FUNCTION

60°   64°   68°   72°   76°   80°   84°

Desirable
Temperature

Figure 8.7
Loss Function Relating to Temperature

The increase of "loss of comfort" escalates at a much more rapid rate between 64 degrees and 60 degrees than between 72 degrees and 68 degrees. The theory suggests that the equal increments of degree loss, 4 degrees in this case, have greater negative impact on larger numbers of people the further you move from the desirable temperature of 72 degrees.

In education, we tend to believe that knowledge and skill acquired by a student can be represented by an assessment score. Also, the assessment score implies equal increments of difference in the amount of knowledge and skill the person has learned. If one student receives a 60 on a test and another student receives an 80, the difference implies a 20 percent differential in knowledge between the students.

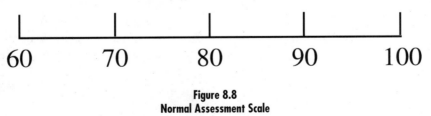

60   70   80   90   100

Figure 8.8
Normal Assessment Scale

The implication expressed in the above assessment scale is that each level of knowledge loss is equal—a 10 percent loss for each 10-point increment down the scale. The loss from 100 to 90 is the same as from 90 to 80 and so on. Even though the numbers of students may follow the normal distribution frequency in the amount of 100s, 90s, 80s, 70s, and 60s, the degree of difference between the scores is viewed as equal horizontal increments. The "loss function" raises a different understanding of this scale, and the implication is significant relative to the instructional response needed.

The loss function is represented by a parabolic curve with the vertex of the curve, the tip, at the desirable expectation for the population. (See Figure 8.9.)

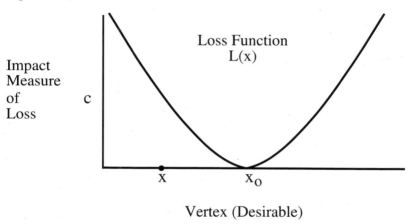

Loss Function $= c(x-x_O)$

c = units of loss on the vertical scale
x = distance away from desirable
x_O = desirable point (vertex of the parabola)
$L(x)$ = impact of the loss function (actual loss)

Figure 8.9
Loss Function Curve

Learning losses do not take place in equal amounts expressed in horizontal distances here but in unequal amounts seen in vertical distance. First of all, the 100 through 60 performance range is normal. However, even scoring this normal distribution, let us look at the loss of measurable knowledge suggested at the 80, 70, and 60 levels of this scoring system. Theoretically, the loss due to these levels is much greater than perceived by most people. In Figure 8.10, 80 is desirable, (x_o), and the impact of loss to the student is represented by the vertical distance, a geometric change, not the horizontal difference shown in the figure, which is linear.

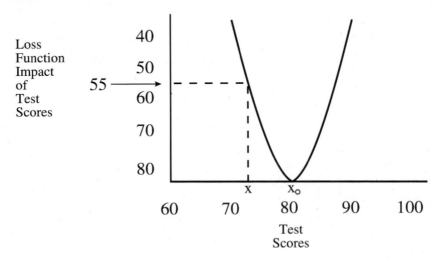

Figure 8.10
Loss Function Impact

The score of 80, desirable, is the "no loss point" on the above scale (x_o). A score of 75 is the student's score, 5 points away from desirable (x). The loss is usually represented by 80 - 75 = 5 units from desirable. However, the loss function suggests that the actual loss is 25 units. A score on the horizontal scale reflects the actual loss on the vertical scale. Therefore, a score of 75 represents a loss function score of 55.

In Figure 8.11, the loss of knowledge is indicated by the vertical lines C1 - C2, D1 - D2, and F1 - F2, rather than by the horizontal lines C0 - C1, D0 - D1, or F0 - F1. The Specification Limits Model suggests equal amounts of loss within an assessment interval. The loss function describes the escalated amount of loss within an assessment interval as the behavior moves further away from desirability. (See Figure 8.10.)

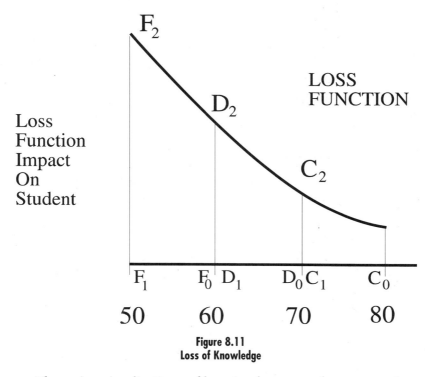

Figure 8.11
Loss of Knowledge

The serious implications of learning losses are demonstrated more graphically by the loss function idea than by any application (or misapplication) of specification limits to education. Learning deficits—those that come about through unavoidable disabilities and those that result simply from students falling behind in the system for any number of other reasons—are more difficult to overcome than people generally imagine. The greater the deficit, the greater the need for extensive intervention to help lagging students become functional. It is important to respond quickly to the needs of any student identified as being below the -3 SD level in a reading system. More instructional time or special instructional strategies might be the answer or whatever it takes to avoid loss for the student in the needed area of learning. In their reliance on Industrial, Specification Limits, and Competitive models of system management, our schools do not really address the impact of the loss function.

SYSTEM IMPROVEMENT

It is critical to clarify the aim of the system in order for people to understand their tasks in the system. Reducing variation is one of the most important elements in system improvement. Reducing variation within a system is decreasing the range between the mean and the ±3 standard deviations. (See Figures 8.12, 8.13, 8.14.)

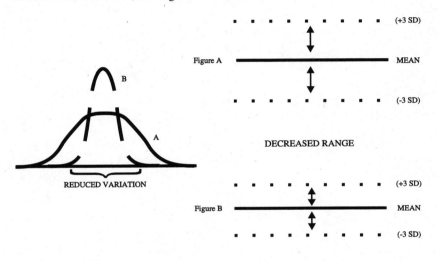

Figure 8.12
Improvement

If in the writing samples of a given group of students the mean number of spelling errors is 10 with a ±3 standard deviation of 5, the error range of the students would be 5 through 15. The second important element in system improvement is improvement of the system average. In this case, the average should decrease to achieve the aim.

Figure 8.13
Intervention Strategy: Improve the Mean and Reduce Variation around It

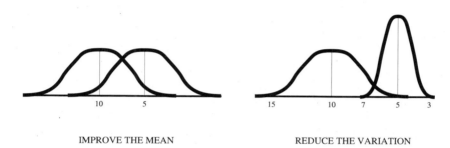

IMPROVE THE MEAN   REDUCE THE VARIATION

Figure 8.14
System Improvement

After instruction, the mean score of spelling errors in this example was reduced from 10 to 5, and the variation of errors around the mean was reduced from 5 to 2.

Initial scores: 10 ± 5 Improved scores: 5 ± 2

System improvement is accomplished by shifting the mean of the group performance toward the desired aim and reducing the variation around it. In this example, both the average number of spelling errors and variation from this point needed to be reduced. The trend observed indicates improvement. The aim, of course, is to eliminate all spelling errors.

Continual improvement of a system integrates all the elements discussed in this chapter: valuing people, understanding a system, normal distribution, statistical control, common and special causes of variation, loss function, and system improvement.

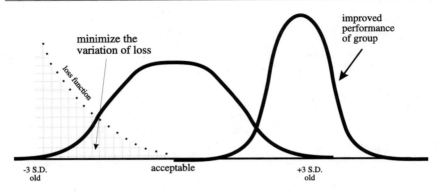

Figure 8.15
Continual Improvement of a System

All of these elements work together to bring about improvement. Each element is interdependently linked to others, and if the aim of the system is to be achieved, they must all move in unison. In an educational system, the aim is to improve the teaching and learning process continually in order to create—or recapture—joy in learning. The question is, how can we improve the school system continually? Dr. Deming asked educators to value people in the system above all else. Create an atmosphere for each person to contribute to the system. Involve people in feedback to improve the system. Understand the clients in the system as well as those who are served by it.

Understanding the system is essential. Define the components of the system, clarify the aim of the system, and make sure everyone understands that aim. Any system must be managed in this way. Likewise, understanding the results of the system is essential. To implement continual improvement strategies, educational leaders must understand concepts such as normal distribution, statistical control, common and special causes of variation, and the loss function. Without understanding and application of these concepts, effective change is impossible.

IMPLICATIONS FOR THE FUTURE

It can be said that the basic school objectives are to make learning enjoyable and to help students develop the attitudes and skills they need to become lifelong learners. To do this, educators need to be persistent in improving the instructional process. But how? According to Dr. Deming,

120

people need to be valued above all else. Educational leaders need to create an atmosphere in which each person can provide feedback and help solve problems. Leaders must also maintain a system perspective. If they can apply basic statistical analysis to their situations, they have an extra tool—one that will help them understand what is really happening. Leaders so equipped often come to see that traditional thinking is a barrier to progress. Because educational systems of the future will handle large numbers of children, special effort will be required to recognize individual differences. In analyzing this process, we keep realizing the validity of certain principles:

- Teachers, students, administrators, and parents should all think of themselves as players on the same team. Everyone's cooperation is essential. Competition in games and sports contests is fine. But life and learning are not games.

- Constant evaluation of individuals instead of the system is meaningless at best, and it can be destructive.

- Normal behavior is represented by 100 percent of the dispersion around the mean on any specific task. In other words, "normal" is plus and minus three standard deviations from the mean. If a student's performance is outside this range, special help may be needed, but diversity of behavior in many areas is normal and need not be identified as negative. Diversity should be respected, understood, and addressed as a system. If any special cause of variation from the norm is identified, it needs to be addressed in an appropriate manner to prevent loss. The aim is to improve the system and for each person in it to win—to learn.

REFERENCES

Shewhart, W. (1986). *Statistical method from the viewpoint of quality control.* New York: Dover Publications, pp. 85-86.

Taguchi, G. (1981). *On-line quality control during production.* Tokyo: Japanese Standards Association, p. 139.

Wheeler, D.J., and Chambers, D.S. (1992). *Understanding statistical process control* (2d ed.). Knoxville, TN: SPC Press, p. 146.

Joy on the job comes not so much from the result, the product, but from contribution to optimization of the system in which everybody wins.

W. Edwards Deming

CHAPTER 9

CONTINUAL IMPROVEMENT
STEPS AND STRATEGIES

No matter how talented an individual is, he or she is still part of a system. This is illustrated by a conversation Coach Phil Jackson of the Chicago Bulls had with Michael Jordan, the greatest basketball player of our time. The Bulls had finished another season and Michael had received another "Best Player" award. Jackson asked Jordan if he just wanted to keep winning this award, or if he wanted to win the NBA Championship. Jordan was frustrated about not winning it, so Jackson went on to discuss how more teamwork and support from Jordan on the floor would help win the coveted championship. Jackson suggested that Michael be more than an individual winner—that he become a key member of a winning team. The result? Three consecutive NBA Championships!

Each of us is part of many systems: family, religious group, educational setting, governmental group or political party, club, hobby group, sports organization, and more. School systems have many subsystems. There are the elementary, middle school or junior high, and high school grade levels. There are administration, maintenance, and food service sectors. There are subject-area divisions such as music and sports. Everything we do is within a system of some kind. The workings of some systems may not be clear to everyone in them, but the people involved are indispensable. As I have often said, when people feel free to participate in all aspects of system improvement, their service improves. People are nearly always willing to offer information, make changes, try new ideas, and work together if they feel the focus is on system improvement and not them. If leaders dwell on personal performance, workers' intrinsic motivation will be diminished. Everyone needs to be valued and given opportunities to contribute. Leadership approaches that take this truth to heart are ultimately the most productive.

Leaders in whom these principles are instinctive are the most effective. Yet proven procedures for meaningful change can be outlined and learned.

STEP 1: UNDERSTAND THE SYSTEM

Describe the current system and make a flow chart depicting its elements in relationship to each other. Only in seeing the system illustrated will other people get an idea of how you see the situation. Clarify the system aim. In discussing this, keep client or "customer" needs and concerns foremost in mind. The aim is not to be limited to these, however. It should go beyond such expectations. Develop ideas for improving procedures.

STEP 2: ELIMINATE DELAYS

Determine where service delays are evident. Suggest procedures that can be implemented with minor effort to correct these situations. Make needed action clear through written directions, graphic illustrations, checklists, memos on new procedures, and other communication devices. Redraw the flowchart to reflect these minor adjustments. Make sure all agree that this is the process that does exist now.

STEP 3: IMPROVE THE PROCESS

Review where system improvement can be achieved to serve internal and external "customers." Center decision making at the level of implementation and, as a means of improving the process, eliminate organizational layering or other personnel redundancy. Cut down on paperwork and process time. Eliminate exchanges of information that have no bearing on the system aim. (Process tools such as brainstorming and cause-and-effect charting are effective in troubleshooting or otherwise analyzing a system.)

STEP 4: REDUCE UNACCEPTABLE VARIATION

People, procedures, policies, and work conditions are the most usual sources of service that is out of compliance with the system aim. Retraining is the only way to counteract the efficiency losses involved. First bring the system into statistical control. Then distinguish common from special causes of variance, using control charts to analyze relevant data.

STEP 5: MAKE CHANGES

Determine the appropriate intervention. Implement it. Study the results. Make needed adjustments.

The Plan-Do-Study-Act Cycle is used to continuously improve systems and solve problems.

The Plan–Do–Study–Act Cycle

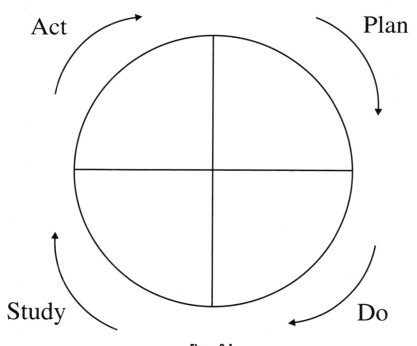

Figure 9.1
PDSA Cycle
(Source: Scholtes, 1990)

PLAN

Clarify present practice.
Develop a theory.
Plan an intervention.
Plan data collection.
Plan assessment procedure.

> What intervention is needed?
> Is the intervention appropriate?
> What steps are needed?
> Who should be involved?
> Whom will the intervention affect?
> What administrative support is needed?
> Who needs to be trained for these?
> Who will supervise the process?
> What data are to be collected?
> How will data be gathered?
> How will they be analyzed?

DO

Educate and train people who will implement changes.
Inform others who will not be directly involved.
Begin in a limited manner or scope.
Determine criteria for assessing the strategy's effectiveness.
Gather assessment data.
Analyze data.

> Where can small procedural changes be made?
> Who needs to be trained to intervene?
> Who will supervise the intervention?
> What data are to be collected?
> How will data be gathered?
> How will data be analyzed?

STUDY

Measure the impact of change.
Compare new data to previous situation.

Perform statistical analyses.
Summarize what is learned.

What does the new information indicate?
What revisions in the strategy might be made?
What aspects of the system are working well and should remain intact?
Is everyone moving in the right direction?
Is the process improving?
What conclusions can be drawn?

Act

Expand new approaches if the picture is positive.
Revise the theory if there are uncertainties.
Reject the strategy if there is no positive change.
Continue improving the process.

Who needs training?
Who needs to be communicated with and included in future planning?
How can application of the strategy be expanded?
What additional resources are needed for continued process improvement?
How can the better process be standardized?
How can continual improvement be assured?

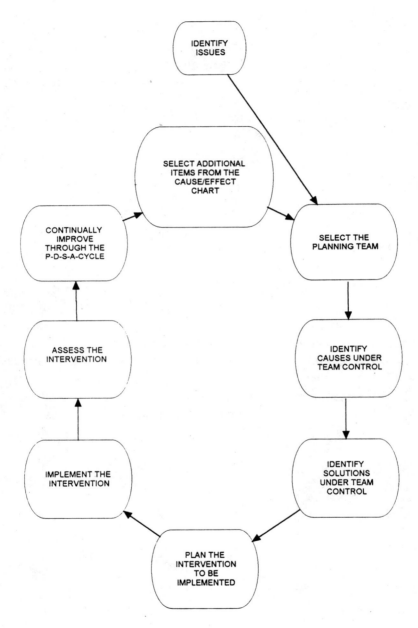

Figure 9.2
PDSA Implementation Steps

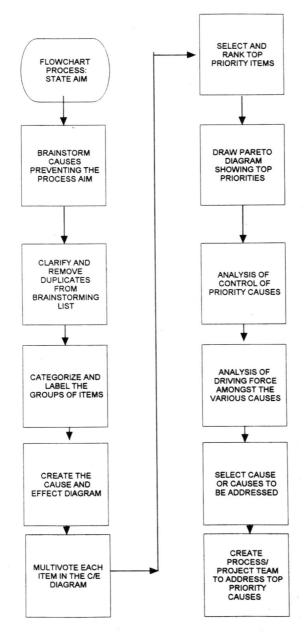

Figure 9.3
STEP ONE: Causes Identification Process

STEP TWO:
PLANNING TEAM SELECTION

1. Who owns the process?

2. What areas should be represented on the team?

3. What is the process for selecting the team?

4. Who should represent each area on the team?

5. When will the team meet?

6. Where will it meet?

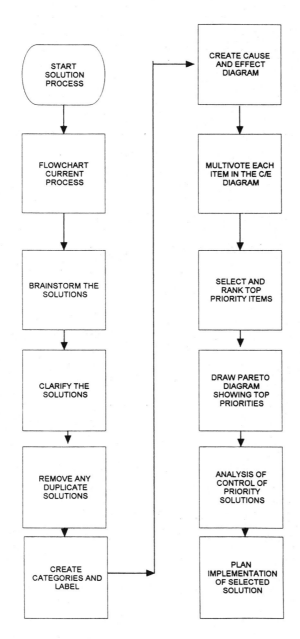

Figure 9.4
STEP THREE: Solutions Identification Process

STEP FOUR:
PLANNING THE SOLUTION

1. Identify the solution intervention to be tested.

2. Who are the people doing the intervention?

3. What training is needed for the intervention?

4. What are the key points to be identified in the process where data need to be collected?

5. How are the data to be collected?

6. How are the data analyzed?

7. How are the data presented to the work group?

8. Who is responsible for decision making as a result of the work-group recommendations, based on the data for process improvement?

9. Redraw the flowchart to illustrate the improved process.

10. Educate the people in the intervention.

11. Plan the time and place for the intervention.

12. Intervene.

STEP FIVE:
IMPLEMENT THE SOLUTION

. . . Do it!

STEP SIX:
ASSESS THE SOLUTION

1. Present that data to the work group.

2. Analyze the data by using control charts.

3. Decide if the intervention improved the process.

4. Based on the analysis, expand the intervention within the workplace or go back to the planning stage and rethink the next intervention for process improvement.

5. Share the process data and future planning with the larger work force to educate and gain support for process improvement.

6. Improve the process forever by continually repeating the six steps.

REFERENCE

Scholtes, P. (1990). *The team handbook.* Madison, WI: Joiner Association, chap. 5, pp. 18-20.

As I see it, the issue is quality—quality of product, quality of service, quality of work environment, and quality of cooperation between government and industry. This nation is at a crossroads in terms of our resolve to recognize and meet the challenge. Transformation is required. Transformation will not be spontaneous.

W. Edwards Deming

CHAPTER 10

THE RIGHT ROAD
TRANSFORMING THE SYSTEM

Dr. Deming developed 14 points that characterize the transformational process. While these points do not constitute the whole of the Deming philosophy, they are important constituents in it. They are vehicles for new thinking. Applied to education, they represent the possibility that there are structurally different and better ways of working with people and organizing instruction.

DEMING'S 14 POINTS:

1. Create constancy of purpose for improvement of product and service.

2. Adopt the new philosophy.

3. Cease dependence on inspection to achieve quality.

4. End the practice of awarding business on the basis of price tag alone. Instead, minimize total cost by working with single suppliers.

5. Improve constantly and forever every process for planning, production, and service.

6. Institute training on the job.

7. Adopt and institute leadership.

8. Drive out fear.

9. Break down barriers between staff areas.

10. Eliminate slogans, exhortations, and targets for the workforce.

11. Eliminate numerical quotas for the workforce and numerical goals for management.

12. Remove barriers that rob people of pride of workmanship. Eliminate the annual rating or merit system.

13. Institute a vigorous program of education and self-improvement for everyone.

14. Put everyone in the organization to work to accomplish the transformation.

APPLICATIONS IN EDUCATION

If we want to bring education in this country to its full capacity, the improvement process must be open to everyone our schools serve. This includes parents and other people in the community. It includes students of every description and capacity. And everyone providing a service needs to be involved, including volunteers and paid staff, cooks and custodians, bus drivers and mechanics, maintenance workers and paraprofessionals, teachers and counselors, record-keepers and financial planners, superintendents and school board members. Yet the central focus must be classroom instruction, for that is where crucial contacts with learners are made. It is where we succeed or fail in the quest for excellence. The heart of the schooling process is instruction. Learning is based on access to that process. The issue we must address is how to open this process so that both internal and external clients of the system can participate in the improvement of instruction. If this does not happen, we fail! Everything else schools do is designed to support the instructional process. We win or lose the war on the system's front line—the interface between teachers and students. This is why I have given major attention to "Instruction as a System."

Instruction as a System

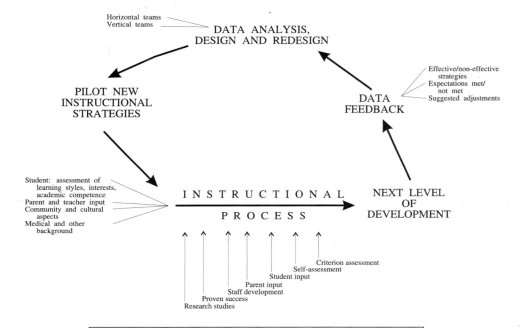

Figure 10.1
Instruction as a System

TRANSFORMATION IN ACTION:
AN APPLICATION OF DR. W. EDWARDS DEMING'S 14 POINTS
TO THE INSTRUCTIONAL SYSTEM

POINT 1

Create constancy of purpose toward improvement of the instructional process, with the aim of enhancing continual growth in knowledge and joy in learning to improve self-development and the society in which we live.

Total concentration on the quality of instruction cannot be accomplished without strong leadership from the top. Educational administrators must have a vision for excellence and take decisive action to make it concrete. This involves constant training and retraining of people. I once heard a man at a wedding dinner tell how he no longer enjoyed being involved in theatrical productions at his church. The plays presented there in the past were somehow better—more beautiful and moving, he felt. Something was missing now. In further discussion with this man, I learned that the church's original purpose in incorporating plays in its ministry was to provide unique opportunities for church members to spend time with each other. It was a simple objective. Now, however, highly talented people were auditioning for and presenting the plays, and some were big productions. As this man and I talked, it became clear to me that church leaders and others involved had lost sight of the aim. Technical perfection had replaced fellowship as a goal.

What is your aim in education? Is it clear to everyone with whom you work? How does it relate to the achievement of instructional excellence?

1.1. Leaders clarify and communicate the aim throughout the school. All actions and decisions are guided by the aim. Any that do not contribute to the achievement of the aim should be rethought.

1.2. Leaders create a collaborative environment in which everyone works together to achieve the goal.

Teachers and administrators of individual schools must meet with parents and community leaders (including representatives of businesses, service clubs, churches, and nonprofit organizations) to clarify shared objectives. If the school does not have a purpose in common with its community, and one that everyone understands, it can't function effectively.

Once when I was a school principal, two students were brought into my office for fighting. A teacher involved in the situation asked that the student who started the fight be dismissed from the school band for a time. The teacher believed this would be a good move because the student enjoyed this "extracurricular" activity. I reminded the teacher of our school aim: "Everything offered is of equal value to the child." According to this principle, a student could not be disciplined by denying access to learning opportunities. It necessitates a new way of thinking about situations calling for corrective action. After a long discussion of alternatives, the teacher and I decided on another disciplinary measure.

POINT 2

Adopt a new philosophy. We are in a new economic age. Leaders must awaken to the challenge, learn their responsibilities, and accept their role of leadership for change.

If we are in a new economic age, leaders everywhere must awaken to the challenge, learn their responsibilities, and accept their role in bringing about meaningful change. The fainthearted or those who expect quick results are doomed to disappointment. Fads such as TQM (Total Quality Management) will pass. They are not to be confused with the Deming philosophy. People are already saying such things as, "We tried these TQM tools, and they do not work." If a management philosophy is not supported by durable beliefs (such as Deming's notion of valuing people at every turn), organizational change is impossible. We choose to walk certain paths in life, hoping to improve the way for others as we travel. Quality is a choice, a commitment to continual improvement—not a feeling. It involves new thinking and long-term commitment.

2.1. Leaders are responsible for learning a new philosophy characterized by cooperation, not competition.

2.2. Leaders create open communication and cooperation between people at all levels of the system through horizontally and vertically integrated teams. Dr. Deming always said self-transformation is the first step on the road to quality. Those who wish to lead others must be examples of self-study and self-awareness, and they must embody the principles of continual improvement.

POINT 3

Cease dependency on inspection to achieve quality. Eliminate the need for inspection on a mass basis by building quality into the implementation of the instructional process.

One eliminates the need for routine, system-wide inspection by building quality into instructional processes. Routine mass testing or evaluation is inefficient and ineffective. Dr. Deming told of a printing company that had its materials proofread by eleven people yet was plagued with errors and customer complaints. None of the readers took the job seriously. Each depended on the others to catch mistakes. To put this another way, no one has ever lost weight by standing on a scale. Mass inspection will not improve the quality of any process. The process must itself be in statistical control. Then, through carefully thought-out strategies initiated by leaders over time, it will improve. How many signatures do we need to approve a financial request? Is any one of these people proofreading the work of any of the others? Building trust and ownership for quality throughout the organization starts with each work group embracing the aim and helping other groups achieve it.

3.1. Criterion-referenced assessment should be standard procedure for analyzing student performance. Students ought not to be simply graded or ranked and left to move through the system in a position thought to be appropriate at any one time. When they acquire knowledge and skill, they should advance to learning opportunities independent of age or grade-level groupings.

3.2. Students' feedback on the instructional process should be valued.

Many believe that simply by setting a higher standard and testing for it, instructional quality will be enhanced. It will not. Quality is achieved through continual improvement, a process that creates both higher standards and the means of attaining them. Setting standards and testing for them yields a lot of numbers but little that is illuminating about the process. Test results tell us where we are in instruction but not how to get where we want to be. A school or school district can satisfy its measurement needs by testing representative samples of students. In this way, thousands of dollars in time and effort can be saved and those resources put to work in better ways. Also, individual scores should not be sent home, because the margins for error on most standardized exams is too large. Testing should be done only to help teachers and administrators understand and improve their instructional system.

POINT 4

Cease the practice of awarding contracts on the basis of price. Instead, minimize total cost and integrate management and learning systems utilizing varied organization and community resources. Internal and external customer needs are considered in determining total cost. Build trust with single suppliers to benefit the entire system.

Build long-term trust with single suppliers of educational goods and services. Always consider value rather than price. Without an adequate measure of quality, business drifts to low bidders, and lesser quality and high cost are the inevitable results.

4.1. Cooperate with other community agencies on coordinating educational programs and cost projections for greater purchasing power.

4.2. Maximize system cost-effectiveness by integrating curricular goals, instructional planning, and material purchasing.

The business manager of one school district with which I have worked bought a quantity of inexpensive copier paper. After the paper was distributed to the schools, copy machines would not work properly because paper was jamming in them. Secretaries were constantly away from phones and their desks, separated from other staff and students, because they had to clean out the machines. The cost in lost time, unanswered phone calls, undelivered services, and upset people was tremendous. There is no way to measure this kind of loss.

POINT 5

Improve constantly and forever the system of management and instruction to improve the quality and productivity of school services and decrease managerial and instructional costs.

Improving a process, wrote Dr. Deming in 1986, means "continual reduction of waste and continual improvement of quality in every activity: procurement, methods, maintenance, location of activities, methods of distribution, accounting, payroll, and services to customers." This is the key to increasing quality and productivity as well as reducing future costs. And the further "upstream" one can go to make improvements, the more everyone benefits. Additional time spent in planning and design of services pays dividends. To extend the water-flow analogy, it is better to prevent water supply contamination than to have to filter the water once it arrives at the point of use. In the organizational context, clarity of function upstream in the flow of services allows for efficient and effective decision making downstream!

5.1. Provide staff leaders with training on statistical control, variation, common cause, and special cause as statistical means of determining where the system needs improvement.

5.2 Implement the "Plan-Do-Study-Act" Cycle.

Teachers need to clarify the aim of the curriculum, identify the key areas of knowledge and skill to be attained by students, assess the situation, and continually improve instruction. Unless they do, nothing changes for the better.

Point 6

Institute training in the workplace. Commitment to staff development is essential for continuous improvement of the instructional process.

People are the most important asset in any organization, yet one of America's greatest failures is its inability to use human resources wisely. New employees need to be oriented to the continual improvement philosophy—if they aren't already—and employees should be taught the philosophy on an ongoing basis. Training should go beyond the boundaries of individual job descriptions, however. Understanding system improvement as it applies to all recipients of educational services is crucial.

6.1. Expert training in how to gather and analyze information is essential.

6.2. Individual student learning styles need to be accommodated.

When a learner is brought into statistical control, introduce different instructional techniques for added improvement. Each new teacher, administrator, staff person, and student should have a mentor, and along with training for new people, ongoing support must be built into the first year. Leaving teachers on their own after a few staff development meetings will not do it! In the district where I worked as an associate superintendent of curriculum and instruction, each school staff had weekly in-service training that lasted an hour and a half. This much staff development time was necessary—in fact, invaluable.

POINT 7

Adopt and institute leadership. Leaders create an environment that enables improvement and change by providing opportunities for each person to learn quality management principles to achieve a quality educational system. Leaders are responsible for taking immediate action on any condition detrimental to the quality of the system.

Management is not supervision but leadership. Leaders create environments in which people can learn quality management principles. Leaders take immediate action on detrimental conditions. Leaders translate designs for improvement into actual improvements. Favorable numerical outcomes are desirable, but if results are a numerical goal, the system will never achieve its full capacity. People will "manufacture" results to meet expectations. If a departmental goal, for example, is to reduce the time of producing reports from 60 to 45 days, it will happen. The quality of the reporting may fall off, but in all probability deadlines will be met. The objectives in this case should be to improve the *quality* of reporting and the time it takes. With respect to the principle of continual improvement, a deadline "day" in itself has little meaning.

7.1. By exemplifying to those they work with the principles of system change, leaders enable people to make significant improvements.

7.2. Leaders should not hold people accountable for system ineffectiveness. Knowing the difference between common and special causes of variation and responding appropriately, effective leaders will emphasize systemic and programmatic development.

Assessment data should be used to identify areas of concern involving expected student learning. Test scores help us revise the curriculum, change the sequence of instruction, improve methods of instruction, and reassess the usefulness of materials.

POINT 8

Leaders drive out fear and encourage two-way communication so everyone can work effectively to achieve the aim of the system. Leaders remove conditions that cause fear of learning, such as competition, reprisal, ridicule, and embarrassment.

Leaders inspire two-way communication so everyone can work together effectively. For the sake of students, teachers, and others in their spheres of influence, leaders eliminate common causes of anxiety, including competition and the possibility of reprisal, ridicule, or embarrassment. Common expressions of anxiety in the workplace include the following:

- I could do my job better if I understood what happens next.

- I am afraid to put forth an idea. My boss may be upset with my idea because it does not agree with his or her idea.

- I am afraid that my next annual rating may not recommend me for a raise.

- I am afraid to admit a mistake.

- I mistrust management. I can't believe what they say when behavior is not consistent with their words.

- I am afraid that I may not always have an answer when my boss asks something.

No one can work well feeling insecure. Leaders in both business and education, however, can establish emotionally secure work environments by treating people in a collegial manner—with genuine respect and camaraderie.

8.1. The goal is mutual trust. Leaders must create an atmosphere in which risks can be taken and mistakes made, in which experimentation is encouraged and a passion for improvement is rewarded.

8.2. Reward systems in education should be based on the idea that everyone gains when the instructional process improves.

Staff and student mentoring services are one way to engender cooperation. A staff and student support network can be designed to help new teachers get acclimated and to address student concerns. An atmosphere of complete acceptance is necessary. The middle school in which I was a principal created a student advisory system in which students could discuss any issue with other students and with an adult who would not be judgmental. Listening with empathy was encouraged. Students knew the group was there to help, not evaluate. The adult's role was to assure that the student's position was expressed and understood if the matter concerned another adult in the school.

POINT 9

Break down barriers between administrative units, departments, and subject-matter disciplines. Leaders create integrated communication networks at all levels of the system to improve the instructional process and maintain the students' yearning for learning. Integration of various processes is designed to optimize the quality of the system. Optimization of any component that minimizes the learning opportunity of a student is questioned and re-thought in terms of the aim of the system.

To improve instruction and maintain students' yearning for learning, school administrators should create integrated communication networks at all levels. Various processes can often be combined to good effect. Optimization of any component that diminishes learning opportunity, however, should be questioned.

Departments must work together. Workers from different areas need to solve common problems. People in research, design, and purchase of materials, for example, ought to meet regularly with representatives of subject areas on matters of mutual interest. Barriers to cooperation and progress come in many forms: poor communication, misunderstandings, unclear objectives or policies, competition, pressure from quota systems, and interpersonal tensions. When leaders set up cross-functional problem-solving teams, however, they are taking a step in the right direction.

9.1. Create "Quality Improvement Teams" to gather and analyze data on various processes, taking advantage of both horizontal and vertical linkages among people in the system.

9.2. The key to improving instruction is a team focus, applying "profound knowledge" in problem areas.

When teachers create interdisciplinary thematic units of study, they come to respect each other's knowledge, perspective, abilities, and unique contributions to a new and greater whole. And students benefit from the process. For example, a varied grouping of students and teachers consider an actual design for a school building from the perspective of people with disabilities. How would special needs be addressed architecturally? How could different areas of study be brought to bear on such a project? Student and faculty teams could study the physical limitations involved and come up with solutions, being aware of federal and state laws and local ordinances. They might visit buildings that provide good and bad examples of accommodation to persons with disabilities. They could hear presentations from people with limited mobility or who are otherwise physically challenged. They could present position papers and examples of projects, give each other feedback and learn from one another. Previously unrecognized barriers between people might be broken down in the process. It would be a good learning scenario.

POINT 10

Eliminate slogans and targets that create the pressure to do quality work without the means to do so from leadership. Such unrealistic expectations increase adversarial relationships. The bulk of the causes of low achievement are inherent in the system and lie beyond the power of the staff to change them.

Catch phrases and performance targets create the pressure for quality work without providing the means to attain it, and unrealistic expectations tend to foster adversarial relationships. Most causes of low achievement are inherent in the system. Some are beyond the ability of school personnel to change. Leaders need specific goals for themselves, but to convert these to numerical destinations for others without furnishing road maps can have effects that are the opposite of those sought. The message may appear to be that administrators are dumping their responsibilities on teachers and others in the system. This can generate frustration and resentment. Your work is your self-portrait. Would you sign it? No—not when you are given defective materials, poor training, and improper information, or when you are not involved in decisions that affect you and yet are expected to produce results. Quotas and numerical goals need to be replaced with statistical methods of analyzing problems, combined with teamwork and trust.

10.1. Achievement quotas won't work in and of themselves. Establishing ways for people to gather information, interpret it, and improve teaching processes based on reasonable conclusions—that will work.

10.2. A good educational system focuses on systemic opportunities for positive change among students, teachers, administrators, parents, and community members—not on individual blame for system shortcomings.

We need to create systems that provide opportunities for people to reach their full capacity. Numerical objectives and slogans have little to do with this. Admittedly, "Value everyone" is a slogan, but it is not a quota statement, and the good situation it implies is attainable. Whenever we make measurement into the most valued aspect of learning, we lose ground.

When the focus is on system improvement, the results take care of themselves. Here are examples of what I mean:

- Work on a swimming stroke, and lap speed will improve.

- Improve study habits and strategies, and the knowledge and insight increase.

- Perfect the form of free throw shooting, and the ball will go in the basket more often.

- Get people to listen better, and group work is more productive.

- Attentive listening to the opinions people express leads to better understanding of their needs.

Point 11

Eliminate quotas and implement assessment strategies so students can affirm learning and predict their readiness for future instruction, to enable additional learning. Eliminate management by objectives, management by results, management by numbers, and numerical goals for professional staff.

Part A

The loss to American industry from the emphasis on production rates and piecework assessment must be appalling. These are measures of quantity only. A graduate student once told her classmates that an airline for which she worked set a quota of twenty calls per hour for customer service representatives. In these telephone conversations, the service reps were to make plane reservations for callers and answer pertinent questions, being courteous and not appearing to be in a rush. She was often frustrated because the airline computer was slow, and when she did not have needed information, she had to use directories and guides. What was her job? To answer twenty calls per hour? Or to provide good service? Numerical work expectations, Dr. Deming said, are a fortress against improvement of both quality and productivity. The implications for education are clear. We need to eliminate student achievement quotas and assess learners in ways they can understand as indicators of their readiness for future instruction.

11.1. Show students how to improve their ability to investigate, communicate, analyze information, and make decisions. Establish "learning improvement" outcomes and criterion-referenced assessments as measures of student progress.

11.2. Consider standardized assessment systems for data gathering but never for individual student or school evaluation. Constantly analyze data for the purpose of improving instruction. Sampling of large populations should be considered.

PART B

On April 8, 1994, a U.S. Marine found not to be a citizen of the United States was interviewed on the CBS morning news. He was well-decorated, well-respected, and supported by the Marine Corps. "How could this happen?" the marine was asked. He explained that, eleven years before, a Marine Corps recruiter needing to meet an enlistment quota had lied in filling out part of this man's application form. Pressure to meet a number clouded the recruiter's judgment. When the marine was asked why he had come forward with this information, he said was concerned about receiving family benefits and needed to resolve the issue.

Another interesting story is told by a man who worked in a state education office where applications for teacher certification are reviewed. The manager of that office rewards workers on the basis of how many application folders are reviewed. "Reviewed" means making a decision. Any decision—not enough data available, proper data but not meeting criteria for approval, approval after review—is appropriate. Some folders require a lot of time and effort to review. Others take only a few minutes.

The man says he would come in early on Mondays and scan the folders needing attention that week. He would select the easiest cases for review, put them on his desk, and leave the more difficult applications for other employees to process. He did this for months, and no one suspected anything. And while *he* was rewarded with bonus pay, another employee, who got many difficult cases to work on, was reprimanded for being slow. Numerical quotas can destroy employee morale, motivation, and pride in workmanship. The numbers approach is a poor substitute for managers taking responsibility for system improvement. By the way, to my knowledge, the quota system is still in effect in the office just described.

11.3. Eliminate all forms of management by objectives, results, or numbers for professional staff. Train teaching leaders to use statistical strategies to improve instruction process rather than to evaluate staff members.

11.4. Base professional advancement on interpersonal skills, demonstrated proficiency in statistical analysis, and the desire to acquire new knowledge consistent with system quality.

POINT 12

Remove barriers that keep pride of workmanship from staff and students.

PART A

People normally take pride in their work. In some situations, however, workers and managers alike are regarded as commodities and treated accordingly. Instead of being involved in decisions that affect them, they are disenfranchised. They may also be faced with poor working conditions. Workers need good equipment and defect-free materials, proper supervision and training, good communication, and a positive, problem-solving atmosphere. In the absence of these resources, they can hardly be expected to do their best. Business owners and top managers who accept poor quality as a way of life deprive themselves and their workers of a powerful source of motivation: the personal pleasure of seeing a job well done. The same is true of educational leaders.

12.1. Abolish annual ratings, management by results, end-of-the-year staff evaluations, and performance reviews for individuals.

12.2. Create a system in which teachers can support and mentor each other with the overall aim of instructional excellence.

12.3. Reward teachers who conceive and implement outstanding ideas for student work.

PART B

Much of what students are required to do is of questionable value. Student assignments should be interesting and enjoyable and at the same time be focused on the development of knowledge or skill. In the area of English instruction, for example, it seems to me that writing a novel would be a great idea. A teacher could demonstrate writing skills, and students could compose stories over the course of a school year, sharing portions of them from time to time with their classmates. In this way, they could help each other, offering wording suggestions and ideas for plot, character, and theme development. By the end of the year, all academic expectations for novel writing would come into play, and there would be tangible results. Do you think these productions would end up on hall floors with all the rest of the papers students empty out of their lockers at year's end? Not likely. In fact, I think projects like this might be read to the family, including grandparents, eventual husbands or wives, eventual children, and eventual grandchildren, and then would be passed on as family treasures to coming generations. Such work would generate justifiable pride of accomplishment, and no letter grades would have to be given. Teachers who attempt it might tire of reading stories, but their joy in touching students and their families in this way would be immeasurable.

12.4. Integrate content objectives into units of study that involve meaningful projects and minimize repetitious tasks. Provide opportunities for students to feel satisfaction in completing work and doing it well.

12.5. Encourage student expression and value student feedback.

POINT 13

Institute a rigorous program of education for professional staff to encourage lifelong learning.

Dr. Deming noted that improvement in productivity means that fewer people may be needed for some lines of work. At the same time, however, more people may be needed in other areas. Education and training fit people into new jobs and new responsibilities. Lifelong learning is truly the rule in this new philosophy. Ideally, everyone is continually growing in the overall effort to improve products and services. Being flexible in knowledge and skills enhances the value of each person for future opportunities.

13.1. Staff commitment to lifelong learning improves instruction.

13.2. Teachers and other professional staff people continue to gain profound knowledge—that is, new knowledge that enables them to improve the system.

Each school should establish ongoing professional-growth seminars. Continual learning cannot be optional.

POINT 14

Transformation of an organization to improve the quality of instruction is everyone's aim. Everyone wins in a learning community that collectively and cooperatively transforms the system to achieve the aim.

System change should be everyone's aim. It is top administrators, however, who must feel pain and dissatisfaction with past performance and have the courage to move in new directions. They must see their need to break out of the existing system, even to the point of risking peer disapproval, so that a "critical mass" of people in the system can come to understand continual improvement in thought and methodology. When this happens, people become convinced that what they are doing is right. Everyone begins to work together. Gradually and in small steps, the system is seen and felt to be on the move. Quality goes up. Everyone wins!

14.1. Leaders are responsible for the professional growth of people in the system and for encouraging cooperation at all levels.

14.2. Leaders provide the vision for change. Others implement it. Students gain. Communities benefit.

THE BIG PICTURE

What is required in all of this is a passion for quality, a mindset that "good" is not good enough. If we decide anything is good enough, we have given up on making it better. Certain things might be good enough, but the educational system in this country is *not* good enough for more than half of the students it claims to serve. Even those who feel the system is doing fairly well, I would venture to say, do not understand the level of quality needed to prepare today's children for the 21st century. What we are teaching today is not addressing the issues of diversity in the world. We need to value all people everywhere and learn, for survival's sake, to cooperate with each other. In the interest of our children, grandchildren, and great-grandchildren, we have much to do—and so much to learn.

Transformation into a new style of [leadership] is required to successfully respond to the myriad changes that shake the world. . . . Transformation is not automatic. It must be learned; it must be led.

W. Edwards Deming

CHAPTER 11

A CHALLENGE FOR LEADERS
TRANSFORMING SELF AND OTHERS

As a father, I am to lead by example. As a leader, I am to walk my talk. As a teacher, I am to model what I believe. In all these roles and responsibilities, it starts with me. The first step is mine! Leaders must internalize the idea of continual improvement before trying to influence anyone else.

For some educational administrators, perhaps, the changing of personal thought patterns will be a first step. Leadership is responsible for creating the environment for continual improvement of any system. People working in the system must be valued and involved in the system-improvement process. Leadership is the key mental shift involved in the Deming philosophy. It is what enables one to focus on improvement methods and system results. Continual learning and study is involved as well. Experience or longevity in position is not enough. Inspiring leaders are those who constantly challenge current theories and create new ones to be tested. Experience analyzed in the crucible of predictions based on hypotheses is the basis of significant knowledge.

I suggest that anyone interested in improving education read Dr. Deming's latest book, *The New Economics*. It would be good, as well, to view videotapes of Dr. Deming's four-day seminar. Films Incorporated in Chicago provides access to the Deming Library. (See Recommended Reading for related resources.) Study carefully what Deming says before going into other material on educational reform. Don't be misled or misinformed. Many people have written about "total quality management" (TQM) as it applies to education but have not addressed the system of continual improvement or the philosophy of profound knowledge. I believe most writers have not fully understood Dr. Deming's teachings. Many have addressed his 14 Points and applied them in various ways. One rarely sees the underlying philosophy explained, however. You need to be discerning.

From this book and selected others, you will see a new portrait of educational leadership emerging. Those who feel called to guide our school systems into meaningful change will be people of varying backgrounds and temperament, but they will have traits and abilities in common. For example, they will . . .

SEE CLEARLY

Each school is a unit of change. The values of a community are taught and transmitted through it. Thus community and school leaders must come to a shared vision of excellence. Then they must go into partnership to implement it. This puts everyone on a single team. Nonetheless, the primary responsibility of school leaders is to work on their systems. They need to educate teachers in group-process skills and decision making, for when people do not work well together they waste time, and the cause of system reform is set back. Only leaders can pull everyone in the system into the process. Improvement cannot be left to voluntary action. It is required of everybody.

BE TEAM PLAYERS

As specific areas are zeroed in on for improvement, leaders need to form planning teams and educate them in improvement principles, particularly the Plan-Do-Study-Act cycle. Leaders cannot delegate this activity. They must be on these teams. A group of teachers without front-office leadership representation compromises both efficiency and morale. As groups come up with ideas, the role of leaders is to support pilot studies and experimental programs. Once these are under way, the teams will analyze the new data to determine the results of new approaches. A team may no longer be needed in a given area if the process improves. In that case, it can move on to other areas. Only as different improvement strategies are implemented and tested will benefits to students become clear. Planning for improvement never ends. Teams and team members, projects and processes may change, but the continual improvement process is just that—continual!

SHOW GENUINE SUPPORT

Such teams need a lot of encouragement. Administrators need to be sources of optimism and good cheer. They need to be enthusiastic. They need to affirm individuals and help groups acquire the material and financial resources they need. If a staff sees that a particular strategy is not productive, a different tack should be taken, of course. Leaders must support this challenging process of searching with a combination of tenderness and firm resolve.

MAKE STATISTICAL CHECKS

Statistical tools help educators know if they are making headway in the challenge. Based on reliable data, decisions can be made for additional planning that might be needed to expand a proven intervention or create new ones. Without documented experience, however, teachers and administrators can easily make ill-advised decisions. Sometimes tampering will undo success. Leaders are responsible for teaching staff members to distinguish between common and special causes of variation in the system. If leaders don't know the difference themselves, ignorance determines the next move. This can be disastrous. We all pay for ignorance.

UNIFY THROUGH UNDERSTANDING

Leaders pull everything together. To build the kind of relational bridges they need, leaders must understand that teachers, as well as students, learn in different ways and at varying rates. They have different personalities and values. Some are more adept socially than others. This does not mean they are to be valued differently. A person's worth should never be in question. Effective leaders create environments in which each person can make gains on a continual basis.

TAKE CHARGE

Leaders must use the power of position. If they are not willing to exert themselves to change a faulty process, who else can do it? The best way for leaders to effect change, however, is not to clamp down on people but to liberate them to find their true capacity. The impetus for change of this nature has to come from the top down—from the board room to the classroom. The Deming process requires total commitment, dedication, and professional growth, but the payoff is transformational. Properly applied, this philosophy will effect positive change in the lives of leaders and all with whom they work.

We have grown up in a climate of competition between people, teams, departments, divisions, pupils, schools, universities. We have been taught by economists that competition will solve our problems. Actually, competition, we see now, is destructive. It would be better if everyone would work together as a system, with the aim for everybody to win. What we need is cooperation and transformation to a new style of management.

W. Edwards Deming

PERSONAL REFLECTIONS
BELIEF AND COMMITMENT

Late in 1993, it came to my attention that Dr. Deming was not in good health. I wanted to share with him the growing number of educational organizations beginning to focus on his continual improvement philosophy, so I wrote to him. Even in his last days, Dr. Deming took time to send me a note of thanks and support. I am glad that news of this progress elevated his spirits. Although Dr. Deming passed away one month later, his work will live on through those who study and implement his philosophy. To me, Dr. Deming's paraphrase of Ecclesiastes captures the spirit of this message:

Each person is to take joy in one's labor and enjoy the fruits of one's labor. This is true for all people. This is a gift from God.

Ecclesiastes 2:24-26 and 3:12-13

I believe the fruits of Dr. Deming's labor are indeed a gift. If you choose to take the less-traveled road they represent, the joy you experience will be greater than you can imagine. I wish you well and hope we meet along the way.

W. Edwards Deming, Ph.D.
CONSULTANT IN STATISTICAL STUDIES

WASHINGTON 20016
4924 BUTTERWORTH PLACE
———
TEL. (202) 363-8552
FAX (202) 363.3501

20   November   1993

Dear Warwick,

   Your cordial letter, not dated, elevates my spirits.   I wish for you all things good, and remain

                              Sincerely yours,

                              N. Edwards Deming

To Dr. Ron Warwick
     940 Port Clinton Court West
     Buffalo Grove, Illinois
          60089

REFERENCES AND RECOMMENDED READING

REFERENCES USED IN THE TEXT

Council of the Great City Schools (1994). *New York Times*, September 28, pB, 8(N), pB 8(L), column 3.

DeLauder, W. (1992). *Renewing public dialogue: 1992 education agenda.* Denver, CO: Education Commission of the States.

Deming, W.E. (1993). *The new economics for industry, government, and education.* Cambridge, MA: MIT Center for Advanced Engineering Study.

———— (1989). Speech in Osaka, Japan.

Deming Library (1991). Videotape, XVI.

Drucker, P. (1969). *The age of discontinuity.* New York: Harper & Row.

The Economist (1992). November 21, p. 8.

Gardner, D.P., et al. (1983). *A nation at risk.* Washington, DC: The National Commission on Excellence in Education.

Hellriegel, D., Slocum, J., and Woodman, R. (1992). *Organizational behavior* (6th ed.). St. Paul, MN: West Publishing.

Johnson, A.K. (1994). *High school dropouts: 1982-1994.* Chicago Public Schools, Department of Research, Evaluation and Planning, December 19.

Leonard, J.F. (1991). "Applying Deming's principles to our schools." *South Carolina Business*, 11, pp. 82-87.

Leonard, J.F. (1992). *Essential statistical methods for total quality schools.* 79 Cady Lane, Woodstock, CT 06281.

McGregor, D.M. (1985). *The human side of the enterprise* (2d ed.). New York: McGraw-Hill.

Moen, R.D. (1989). "The Deming philosophy for improving the educational process." Paper presented to the Third Annual International Deming Users' Group Conference in Cincinnati, Ohio (8/22/89), pp. 1-24.

Report of Chicago Public Schools achievement trends: October 26, 1994 (1994). Chicago: Chicago Public Schools, Department of Research, Evaluation and Planning.

Riley, R.W. (1994). *The condition of education 1994.* Washington, DC: U.S. Department of Education, National Center for Education Statistics.

Scherkenbach, W.W. (1991). *Deming's road to continual improvement.* Knoxville, TN: SPC Press, p. 64.

Scholtes, P. (1990). *The team handbook.* Madison, WI: Joiner Association, chap. 5, pp. 18-20.

Shewhart, W. (1986). *Statistical method from the viewpoint of quality control.* New York: Dover Publications.

Taguchi, G. (1981). *On-line quality control during production.* Tokyo: Japanese Standards Association, p. 139.

USA Today (1994). February 1, Section D, pp. 1-2.

Wheeler, D.J., and Chambers, D.S. (1992). *Understanding statistical process control* (2d ed.). Knoxville, TN: SPC Press.

RECOMMENDED READING

Aguayo, R. (1991). *Dr. Deming.* New York: Simon & Schuster.

Amsden, D., Butler, H., and Amsden, R. (1991). *SPC simplified for services: Practical tools for continuous quality improvement.* White Plains, NY: Quality Resources.

Amsden, R., Butler, H., and Amsden, D. (1989). *SPC simplified: Practical steps to quality.* White Plains, NY: Quality Resources.

Backaitis, N. (1990). *Managing for organizational quality.* San Diego: Navy Personnel Research and Development Center.

Beckhard, R., and Pritchard, W. (1992). *Changing the essence.* San Francisco: Jossey-Bass.

Collins, J., and Porras, J. (1994). *Built to last.* New York: HarperBusiness.

Covey, S. (1990). *The seven habits of highly effective people.* New York: Simon & Schuster.

——————— (1991). *Principle-centered leadership.* New York: Summit Books.

Crawford, D., Bodine, R., and Hoglund, R. (1993). *The school for quality learning.* Champaign, IL: Research Press.

Delavigne, K., and Robertson, J. (1994). *Deming's profound changes: When will the sleeping giant awaken?* Englewood Cliffs, NJ: PTR Prentice Hall.

Deming, W.E. (1986). *Out of the crisis.* Cambridge, MA: MIT Center for Advanced Engineering Study.

——————— (1993). *The new economics for industry, government, and education.* Cambridge, MA: MIT Center for Advanced Engineering Study.

Dobyns, L., and Crawford-Mason, C. (1994). *Thinking about quality.* New York: Time Books/Random House.

Fellers, G. (1992). *The Deming vision: SPC/TQM for administrators.* Milwaukee: ASQC Quality Press.

Gabor, A. (1992). *The man who discovered quality.* New York: Penguin Books. Reprint, New York: Random House, 1990.

Gardner, H. (1991). *The unschooled mind.* New York: BasicBooks.

Gitlow, H., and Gitlow, S. (1987). *The Deming guide to quality and competitive position.* Englewood Cliffs, NJ: Prentice-Hall.

Gitlow, H. (1990). *Planning for quality, productivity, and competitive position.* Homewood, IL: Dow Jones-Irwin.

Glasser, W. (1985). *Control theory.* New York: Harper & Row.

——————— (1990). *The quality school.* New York: Harper & Row.

Hammer, M., and Champy, J. (1993). *Reengineering the corporation.* New York: HarperBusiness.

Hoy, W., and Miskel, C. (1991). *Educational administration* (4th ed.). New York: McGraw-Hill.

Ishikawa, K. (1986). *Guide to quality control.* Tokyo: Asian Productivity Organization.

——————— (1989). *Introduction to quality control.* (2d rev. ed.) Tokyo: USE Press.

Joiner, B. (1994). *Fourth generation management: The new business consciousness.* New York: McGraw-Hill.

Kohn, A. (1986). *No contest: The case against competition.* Boston: Houghton Mifflin.

——————— (1993). *Punished by rewards: The trouble with gold stars, incentive plans, A's, praise, and other bribes.* Boston: Houghton Mifflin.

Mann, N. (1989). *The keys to excellence.* (3rd ed.) Los Angeles: Prestwick Books.

Neave, H. (1990). *The Deming dimension.* Knoxville, TN: SPC Press.

NTL (1988). *Teambuilding.* San Diego: University Association.

Rosander, A. (1991). *Deming's 14 points applied to services.* Milwaukee: ASQC Quality Press.

Ryan, K., and Oestreich, D. (1991). *Driving fear out of the workplace.* San Francisco: Jossey-Bass.

Savary, L.M. (1992). *Creating quality schools.* Arlington, VA: American Association of School Administrators.

Scherkenbach, W. (1991). *Deming's road to continual improvement.* Knoxville, TN: SPC Press.

——————— (1986). *The Deming route to quality and productivity.* Milwaukee: ASQC Quality Press.

Scholtes, P. (1990). *The team handbook.* Madison, WI: Joiner Association.

Senge, P. (1990). *The fifth discipline.* New York: Doubleday/Currency.

——————— (1994). *The fifth discipline fieldbook.* New York: Doubleday/ Currency.

Shewhart, W. (1986). *Statistical method from the viewpoint of quality control.* New York: Dover Publications. Reprint, 1939.

Tribus, M. (1989). *Development flow charting workbook.* Los Angeles: Quality and Productivity.

Walton, M. (1986). *The Deming management method.* New York: Putnam Group.

Wheeler, D.J., and Chambers, D.S. (1992). *Understanding statistical process control* (2d ed.). Knoxville, TN: SPC Press.

Wheeler, D. (1993). *Understanding variation: The key to managing chaos.* Knoxville, TN: SPC Press.

United States Department of Education (1991). *America 2000.* Washington, DC: GPO.

LIST OF FIGURES AND LOCATION

CHAPTER 9

CHAPTER 10

DEMING'S 14 POINTS
APPLIED TO ANY ORGANIZATIONAL SYSTEM

POINT 1:   Create constancy of purpose toward improvement of the educational system, with the aim of providing quality service to the school professional staff.

        Provide research services.
        Provide staff development services.
        Provide material analysis services.
        Provide placement services.

POINT 2:   Adopt a new philosophy. Leaders create the climate for change through cooperation of horizontally and vertically integrated teams within the educational system.

        Create communication networks.
        Conduct needs assessments.
        Educate leaders in the new philosophy.
        Serve schools, do not control them.

POINT 3:   Cease dependency on inspection to achieve quality. Eliminate the need for inspection on a mass basis by building quality into management and implementation of the services.

        Eliminate end-of-the-year staff evaluation.
        Evaluate process.

Establish short- and long-term goals.
Provide staff development on quality principles.

POINT 4: **Cease the practice of awarding contracts on the basis of price. Instead, minimize total cost and integrate management systems utilizing various organizations and community resources. Internal and external customer needs are considered in determining total cost. Build trust with single suppliers to benefit the entire system.**

Assess total system cost.
Assess function and cost-effectiveness.
Establish service priorities for schools.
Work with single suppliers.

POINT 5: **Improve constantly and forever the system of management of services to improve the quality and effectiveness of school services and decrease costs.**

Long-term planning.
Design vertical teams for input.
Design horizontal teams for input.
Design employee feedback systems.

POINT 6: **Institute training in the workplace. Continuous training of all professional staff is required on information-gathering strategies and analysis of information relative to improving service to the schools.**

Provide professional development for staff.
Provide mentoring programs.
Create integrated function teams.
Create integrated analysis feedback.

POINT 7: **Institute leadership. Leaders create an environment that enables improvement and change by providing opportunities for each person to learn quality management principles to achieve a quality educational service system. Management is responsible for taking immediate action on any condition detrimental to the quality of the system.**

Provide educational opportunities.
Encourage cooperation.
Require cross-function analysis.
Require total-system cost analysis.

POINT 8: **Leaders drive out fear and encourage two-way communication so everyone can work effectively to achieve the aim of the system. Leaders remove conditions that cause fear (such as competition, reprisal, ridicule, and embarrassment) and create a safe environment for growth.**

Eliminate end-of-the-year review.
Evaluate service process.
Eliminate rating and ranking of employees.
Sub-optimize part ownership in a process.

POINT 9: **Break down barriers between administrative units and departments. Leaders create integrated communication networks at all levels of the system to enhance the service function for the schools. Integration of various processes is designed to optimize the quality of the system. Optimization of any element that minimizes the service productivity for the schools is questioned and rethought in terms of the aim of the system.**

Optimize the system service.
Integrate analysis of service across function.
Clarify aims and goals and services to meet them.
Reward overall service outcomes and cost-effectiveness.

POINT 10: **Eliminate slogans and targets that pressure quality work without the means to do so. Such unrealistic expectations increase adversarial relationships. Causes of low-quality service are inherent to the system and lie beyond the power of any part of the system.**

Respect the worker.
Trust the worker.
Improve process with a clear aim.
Create cooperation, not competition.

POINT 11: **Eliminate quotas and work standards for the services that need to be provided. Eliminate management by objectives, management by results, management by numbers, and numerical goals.**

Analyze process, not end results.
Constant improvement, not quotas.
Keep eye on the ball, not the scoreboard.
Establish goals, not numerical goals.

POINT 12: **Remove barriers that keep pride of workmanship from all service staff. The responsibility of service staff must change from product to process quality.**

Eliminate merit systems.
Establish new promotion criteria.
Reward cooperative contribution.
Reward integrated functional risk.

POINT 13: **Institute a vigorous program of education and self-improvement.**

Reward any and all educational programs.
Provide on-site educational opportunities.
Encourage learning.
Reward loyalty to the organization.

POINT 14: **Transform the district organization to improve the quality of service to all schools in the system. Everyone wins in a learning community system which continuously improves service and instructional processes, forever!**

Leadership clarifies the aim of the organization.
Leadership improves the system.
Leadership understands variation.
Leadership responsibility is quality.

DEMING'S 14 POINTS
APPLIED TO ANY SYSTEM

The 14 Points are general principles that apply the theory of continual improvement and the system of profound knowledge. Any system can be improved if it is defined and clarified and the aim is agreed upon. With these initial steps taken, our understanding of the 14 Points starts us on the journey to continual improvement.

POINT 1:   **Create constancy of purpose for improvement.**

> Define and clarify the system.
> Clarify the aim.
> Communicate the aim.
> Guide all action by the aim.
> Create a collaborative environment.
> Structure interdependence in the organization.
> Reward based on achievement of the aim.
> Commit to quality.

POINT 2:   **Adopt a new philosophy.**

> Learn the new philosophy.
> Walk your talk.
> Create cooperation, not competition.
> Create cross-functional teams.
> Create horizontal and vertical communication.
> Commit to action based on profound knowledge.

POINT 3: **Cease dependence on inspection to achieve quality.**

Use criterion-referenced assessment.
Use project and portfolio examples.
Eliminate rating and ranking of students.
Achieve levels of competency.
Value students in instructional process.
Cooperate with staff to improve instruction.
Reduce variation by going "upstream."
Recognize that inspection does not improve quality.
Remember that "putting out fires" does not improve quality.
Improve method to improve quality.

POINT 4: **Cease awarding contracts based on price alone.**

Cooperate with other areas and organizations.
Establish long-term relationships, single suppliers.
Integrate planning.
Analyze total cost of process.
Buy on value, not price.

POINT 5: **Constantly improve the process.**

Implement the Deming Cycle: PLAN-DO-STUDY-ACT.
Go "upstream" to improve quality.
Plan prevention first, not only firefighting.
Improve forever; good is not good enough.
Analyze statistical data.
Understand common and special causes of variation.

POINT 6: **Institute training.**

Provide expert training needed.
Respect different learning styles.
Understand the job—system, aim, and method of
improvement.
Remove roadblocks to learning.

POINT 7:   **Adopt and institute leadership.**

Teach all profound knowledge.
Teach all statistical thinking.
Optimize the system.
Create interdependence.
Coach and counsel, do not judge.
Create joy in work.
Understand variation.
Avoid tampering.
Understand cooperation.
Improve the system using position power.

POINT 8:   **Drive out fear.**

Create mutual trust.
Optimize the system.
Educate people.
Eliminate fear, which comes from blaming people.
Remove insecurity to allow creativity.
Reward cooperation.

POINT 9:   **Break down barriers between staff areas.**

Integrate different areas.
Establish common goals, which bring optimization.
Eliminate competition, which causes barriers.
Create cross-functional teams.

POINT 10:   **Eliminate slogans and targets.**

End quotas, which cause sub-optimization.
Work on process.
Assess the process continuously for improvement.

POINT 11:   **Eliminate numerical quotas, management by objectives, management by results**

Eliminate quotas because they do not improve quality.
Improve the process, results will come.
Understand variation.

Set new expectations for advancement.
Eliminate management by objectives.
Manage process, not results.

POINT 12: Remove barriers to pride of workmanship.

Integrate curricular objectives.
Adopt a thematic approach.
Make quality assignments.
Develop cooperative teams for learning.
Implement project-centered learning.
Value student and staff for instructional improvement.
End performance evaluation, annual ratings, and ranking of students and staff.
End grading on normal distribution; respect normal variation.
Remember competition destroys cooperation; school and work are not games.

POINT 13: Institute education for all.

Institute lifelong learning.
Study a new philosophy.
Don't be satisfied with "good"; good is not enough.
Remember that people need to be valued.
Remember that people need to contribute.
Institute continuous improvement.

POINT 14: Transformation to improve quality is everyone's aim.

Educate everyone.
Have the courage to adopt a new philosophy.
Remember that leaders change the system.
Allow everyone to implement improvements within the system.
Allow everyone to benefit from the system.

Passion for quality first requires the understanding that good is not good enough. If we decide anything is good enough, we have decided to give up on making it better. Certain things might be good enough, and the decision to accept them in that state is your choice.

The educational system in this country is not good enough for over 50 percent of the students it claims to serve. Even those families who feel the system is good enough do not understand the quality needed in the system today to meet and exceed the expectations of the 21st century. What we are teaching today is not helping us to address the issues of diversity in the world, valuing all people in the world, cooperating with all people to survive. We have a great deal of improvement to accomplish in order for our children, grandchildren, and great-grandchildren to win in this world.

FIELD REPORTS
TRANSFORMATION IN ACTION

REPORT 1 FROM CHICAGO, ILLINOIS
"ENTHUSIASM FOR LEARNING ECHOES IN HER HALLS"

Thomas Kelly High School, an urban educational center within the Chicago Public School System, District 11, Unit 1400, is located on the southwest side of the city. Nestled among extensive industrial areas and older, single-family and two-flat residences, Kelly serves as an educational oasis for its students and community members. Since Kelly opened its doors in 1928, the spirit and enthusiasm for learning still echo in her halls today. This spirit is reflected in the underlying foundations and premises on which the school continues. Such commitment is clearly stated in the Mission Statement:

> It is the mission of Thomas Kelly High School to provide every student a holistic, qualitative, and rewarding educational experience, in a safe, pleasant, and nurturing environment that will thoroughly prepare them to successfully address the diverse challenges of the 21st century.

HISTORY

Along the route of an early-nineteenth-century Indian trail, which cut across what was then marshlands, stands Kelly High School. Today, that trail, Archer Avenue, provides a major transportation route for its students. Kelly High School was originally a junior high when its doors opened on December 3, 1928. On September 17, 1933, Kelly was one of 10 Chicago junior high schools that was reopened as a senior high school—remaining so to this day.

Kelly was named to honor Thomas Kelly, who came to Chicago in 1861. He entered politics before the town of Brighton Park was annexed to the City of Chicago in 1889. In 1913, he was instrumental in having the site for a high school purchased by the Board of Education in the center of the Brighton Park district. He had hoped to see construction begin during his lifetime, but it was not until 14 years after his death that building began.

Brighton Park, the area immediately surrounding Kelly, began to develop after the Great Chicago Fire in 1871. Today, Kelly's irregularly shaped district serves the Brighton Park and McKinley Park communities on Chicago's southwest side.

STUDENT DEMOGRAPHICS

Current demographics reflect quite a diversity among student racial, ethnic, linguistic, and gender characteristics. The school's student population of 1,974 (total district population: 104,547) represents several racial and ethnic heritages: Hispanic (North, Central, and South American); Caucasian (Western and Eastern European); African-American; Asian (Chinese and Filipino). Since neither prerequisites nor auditions are required for elective classes within the Communication Arts Department, it is important to examine the limited English proficiency of 413 students. A large percentage of these students are enrolled in E.S.L. (English as a Second Language); however, these statistics do not reflect the large majority of students who are recent immigrants who do not speak English and have had little formal education.

Kelly's academic, vocational, and club programs encourage the development of intellectual, social, and physical excellence. Students may choose membership in one of the 49 clubs and/or 23 sports teams. Specialized programs set Kelly apart from other high schools. These special characteristics include:

- **Metropolitan Studies: Options for Knowledge Program**: Options is designed primarily for, but not limited to, the college-bound student. This program focuses on all of the academic disciplines that will lead to the development of a holistic individual living in a cosmopolitan society. The program is geared toward the essentials for college entrance.

- **Explorers Program:** Since 1990, Kelly has increased its coeducational Explorer Posts to seven under the auspices of the Boy Scouts of America. Areas include Sea, Law, Computer, Fine Arts, Financial Planning, Science, and Engineering Explorers. Kelly students also participate in an ongoing experimental program, funded through ESEA Chapter 1, in which they engage in activities related to the natural environment and correlated to their academic activities and experiences in school.

- **T.A.P.** (Truancy Alternative Program: At-Risk Students Cooperative Learning and Counseling Programs): Cooperative learning centers provide academic support services for high-risk students as they continue to participate in regular classroom instruction. Tutoring focuses on students' needs as identified by classroom teachers, academic performance, achievement scores, or voluntary self-assessment. Trained students act as tutors and work under the supervision of subject-area specialists and counselors.

- **Special Education Career Programs:** Since September 1993, Kelly junior and senior special education students have participated in the Step Doors Program, funded by the Department of Rehabilitation. During the school day, students are assisted with interview skills and job-related activities in an internship program with Swisshotel.

- **Gifted Programs:** During the school year, advanced placement is offered in English Literature, U.S. History, Studio Art, Chemistry, and Calculus. Eight juniors and seniors participate in off-campus museum programs one half-day a week. Learning about the interactions between an institution and society is stressed. This program is offered through the CPS Division of Gifted and Talented programs.

- **Carl Perkins Fund:** Kelly was awarded a $100,000 grant for its innovative vocational technology program, which has won many awards. This program is rated by the International Technology Association as one of the top 50 industrial education programs in the United States.

- **Academic Decathlon**: Students participating in this competition have netted gold, silver, and bronze medals in 1992 and 1994.

- **School Beautification**: Through a $2,500 grant from Chicago Community Trust, the school's art and vocational education classes are involved in mural drawings, poster contests for area events, and custom-designing banners for Archer and California Avenues.

Kelly High School has enjoyed a long tradition of involvement in the Brighton Park/McKinley Park communities. In addition to the organizations cited above, the school also reaches out into the community through the following:

> Kiwanis Club of Archer Road
>
> Key Club
>
> Local School Council
>
> Kelly Community Council
>
> Kelly Alumni Association
>
> Brighton Park/McKinley Park Community Cluster

CONTINUAL QUALITY IMPROVEMENT: THE DEMING PHILOSOPHY

THOMAS KELLY HIGH SCHOOL

BACKGROUND

Kelly High School has undergone a positive metamorphosis since Dr. John Gelsomino was appointed principal in May of 1990. As a 30-year veteran of the Chicago Public School system, he knew that establishing school security, discipline, and order were the major issues to be addressed. This was accomplished because learning can take place only in an orderly, organized, and nurturing environment. Kelly High School has become that kind of school.

Long acquainted with the work of W. Edwards Deming, Dr. Gelsomino recognized that the Deming principles that have successfully transformed industry could be applied to education. He established a relationship with Dr. Ronald Warwick of National-Louis University, to work an action plan. Dr. Warwick's primary concern was that of commitment by the principal to work the plan over a period of time. Applying the Deming process to any organization requires leadership and a long-range view. It is not a quick fix. With support of the Local School Council, administration, faculty, and staff, Kelly embraced the Deming process of Quality and Productivity in Education.

IMPLEMENTATION

The introduction to Dr. Deming's program began in the fall of 1992. The faculty and staff spent their Thanksgiving holiday immersed in an intensive three-day workshop conducted by Dr. Warwick. In these sessions, an overview of the Deming philosophy, process, and techniques was given.

In June of 1992, a two-day session was spent reviewing and applying the basic tools, including flow charts, brainstorming, fishbone diagrams, Pareto charts, and the Deming cycle. The floor was opened to answer the question, "What is affecting students' performance at Kelly?" By applying the Deming techniques, the teachers agreed that the students were the problem; a follow-up survey of the students said that the teachers were the problem. Few were surprised by the results.

Analysis of hard data is key to the Deming process. A select team of faculty endured a subzero day in January of 1993 to develop computer skills required to support the statistical analysis. The SPC-PC IV statistical package was taught to this group. The aim was to develop the technical expertise to allow future committee endeavors.

In April of 1993, the final orientation seminar was held in preparation for full participation of Quality and Productivity in Education. This session focused on how to define the issues to be resolved through the Quality Process. Using the techniques learned, the faculty agreed "class cutting" by students is a major concern. A heated discussion ensued over what seemed to be a very simple concept: "What is a Cut?" A group of concerned teachers formed Kelly's first Deming committee.

PILOT PROJECT—STUDENT CUTTING

The first committee formed at Kelly High School served as a test bed for continuing to address other issues in the school. The group was formed to respond to one of the issues identified by the general staff—unexcused absence from class, or "cutting." It met for over four months, and the study included interviews with students, teachers, and administrators. Although the findings were broad, we have defined several suggestions that would help in reducing the number of cuts.

FINDINGS

Students representing the entire student body—honor, average, and at-risk students—were selected to serve on the planning team. The students were taught the Deming process, and they used this knowledge in coming to their conclusions. They gave their reasons for cutting as:

> boring classes
>
> teacher inconsistencies in applying the cut policy
>
> ease of leaving the building
>
> going to daytime parties
>
> teacher bias against gang members
>
> lack of support from home
>
> problems in the home
>
> tardies to school being called cuts

The administration and teachers identified the reasons for cutting as:

> data initially gathered being unreliable
>
> lack of parental support for punctuality and school attendance
>
> a pattern of cutting in grammar school

breakdown in detention policy—the system of processing cuts is inconsistent

Cut-Detention system is a deterrent only for good students, not chronic cutters

students often approached in a negative manner

inconsistent implication of student cuts by the classroom teacher

no regular long division time to counsel the students on their cuts

RECOMMENDATIONS

After thoughtful review, the committee selected the following recommendations for Kelly High School:

Apply and carry out policies in a consistent way, starting with the administration.

Automate the processing of attendance and cuts.

Establish consistent data by compiling information.

Have division teachers identify chronic cutters and refer them for special attention.

Establish regular long divisions for special counseling by teachers.

Reestablish PEER mediation program.

IMMEDIATE IMPLEMENTATION

The processing and recording of cuts has been consolidated with the division teachers because the division teacher best knows each student's circumstances. Additional security has been put in place to prevent unauthorized exit. Study of computerized attendance and student database systems is proceeding.

INITIAL RESULTS

Since several of the recommendations of the planning team have been initiated, teachers and administration have noted a drop in cutting.

Students are staying in class and not leaving the building. This may be a result of the increased security in the school.

Local automation of the attendance system remains a challenge. The Chicago Board computer operation is a centrally located mainframe. Information flows only upward, not to the local school. We are evaluating several alternatives, including writing our own cut processing and monitoring program.

SCHOOL-WIDE IMPLEMENTATION, CONTINUING PROGRESS

Fall of 1994 became the time to inaugurate school-wide implementation of the Deming program. In a one-day seminar, the Quality and Productivity in Education process was reviewed by the faculty, staff, and students. As with any school, the mobility of staff requires ongoing training. Students were included in this session to be leaders in working with the student body. Dr. Gelsomino noted that we are embarking on a journey that will lead Kelly High School to new levels of achievement and accomplishment.

The following planning teams were formed:

Parental & Student Involvement

Integration of Bilingual Students into School Life

Student Attendance and Discipline

Special Education Needs for Severe and Profoundly Challenged Students

Learning Outcomes, Assessment, and Curriculum

Instructional Delivery and Documentation

Graduation Rate

Electronic Technology and Application

The goal for this year is to carry out the PLAN-DO-STUDY-ACT cycle. Committees are developing their priorities, and plans are under way to implement them. The emphasis is being placed on the things that we can control.

We have discovered that by working the process, changes happen formally. For example, the technology committee felt that underutilization of computer resources was a priority issue. When classes are scheduled in the computer lab, not all stations are being used. The lab administrator organized teachers so that students are ready to use all available computers. Teachers are cooperating, students are responding, and the lab is running at near capacity. Further, a before-school period has been added to help juniors and seniors in ACT Prep. This was accomplished not by edict, but through cooperation and communication made possible through the Deming Process.

Dr. John Gelsomino
Kelly High School
4100 S. California Avenue
Chicago, IL
Phone: 312-535-4915

REPORT 2 FROM DES MOINES, IOWA
"DR. DEMING SHOWED US THE WAY"

Dr. Deming teaches us about the central importance of understanding a system and the need to be clear about the aim of the system. Education bureaucracies are examples of multifaceted systems, heavily engaged in system-centered activities. As with most traditional bureaucracies, education organizations are built along program, funding, and function lines. Such organizations have long-established methods of operation and organizational cultures. These operating practices and cultures are commonly designed to promote the de facto aim of the organization, which frequently has little to do with the publicly stated aim, i.e., educational services for students.

Traditional bureaucracies exist in environments characterized by strict hierarchies, turf battles, secrecy, fractured or narrowly focused activities, and various programs operating in isolation. Much too often, these efforts of the organization sub-optimize the larger educational system, despite the hard work and benevolent intentions of the people in these organizations.

As Dr. Deming explained, 98 percent of the results of a system are determined by the system itself and not the people in the system. The example below, based on personal experience, is a good case in point.

The organization was engaged in designing and implementing procedures and rules for a new system of standards for schools. This new system would ultimately impact all schools, teachers, and students in the system.

Teams of employees from throughout the organization were gathered to work on different parts of the procedure, as appropriate to their respective duties, e.g., legal, budget, curriculum, testing, etc. The teams were composed of people representing different sections of the organization. They had little experience working in such teams and typically had little contact with each other.

After many months of working together as a team and in smaller subgroups, the team came to an impasse regarding the sequence of steps in the procedure. The conflict divided the team along traditional organizational turf lines. As frustration grew, team leaders and managers from the various units represented on the team started to approach me to request my intervention on their behalf.

As I listened to their appeals, it struck me that each manager was very sure his or her approach to the design of the process was correct. Each blamed the other managers for being stubborn and refusing to give in—and for frustrating the development of the new system. They came to me with similar complaints, rationales, and predictions of missed deadlines and disaster if I did not intervene and make the other managers do it their way.

It should be noted that all involved were very capable, experienced, and committed professionals. One could not find a better team of people to get the job done. I was faced with choosing one side or the other, a position that did not achieve the aim. I reflected on Dr. Deming's work and determined a course of action. He told us the role of a manager of people has many facets, and among them are:

- *A manager understands and conveys to his people the meaning of a system. He explains the aims of the system. He teaches his people to understand how the work of the group supports these aims.*

- *He helps his people to see themselves as components in a system, to work in cooperation with preceding stages and with following stages toward optimization of the efforts of all stages toward achievement of the aim.*

I suspected that the managers and team members were viewing the new system only from the vantage point of their respective work units. As a result, each was building a component of the system—without sufficient insight into other components of the system and without viewing the total system aim. The parable of the six blind men and the elephant came to mind: each blind man felt a different part of the elephant and described a rope, a tree, a wall, etc. So rather than intervene directly, I suggested that each manager develop a flowchart of the process under development. I also suggested that they create the chart with their respective section members and then convene as an entire project team to share their varying perspectives with each other.

The managers, many of whom had some training in the Deming philosophy, instantly saw my point. They skipped the preliminaries and decided as a team to flowchart the process. I did not see them again until they came forward with their final products several months later.

Within the philosophy of continual improvement lie many basic tools and techniques which are helpful in understanding a system. The ability to graphically depict a system, so all can see it at the same time, is a powerful resource. This is particularly important when developing complex procedures that require many specialists in its creation.

Education organizations, as with other large entities, are designed with multiple subunits. These subunits typically strive to achieve maximum levels of autonomy, defined as freedom to operate without being encumbered by other parts of the organization or external forces. This in turn will often cause management to react by delegating authority and responsibility in narrow segments, thus sub-optimizing the system even further. Subunits often see only self-serving aims, which limits their potential to contribute to the greater aim of the entire organization.

Understanding the system and being informed about its component processes are essential steps in moving toward improvement in education. Much of our recent efforts in school reform sub-optimize the system because they are layered—one on top of another. They all start out as "good ideas," but they don't all help. Why?

It is important for organizational members to be able to see the components and how they interact with each other in support of the entire system. It is important for the organization to be clear about its aim. The leader must be ever mindful to ensure that all are informed about the organizational aim.

Continual improvement in education and the achievement of quality education for all students can be accomplished by applying Dr. Deming's philosophy of management. Whether used by a teacher or governor, the tools and techniques available when working with the philosophy offer powerful resources within the context of its philosophical underpinnings. Transformation in education means profound change.

Dr. Deming has shown us a way to gain the knowledge needed to achieve that change through continual improvement.

> Dr. Al Ramirez
> Director: Iowa Department of Education
> Grimes State Office Building
> Des Moines, IA 50319-0146
> Phone: 515-281-3436

REPORT 3 FROM RIVERSIDE, CALIFORNIA
"A PROPHET IN OUR OWN LAND"

I'm a Saab buff. I restore classic cars and have followed the auto industry for years. I first became aware of Dr. W. Edwards Deming when he became a prophet in our own land, through his significant impact on the auto industry. This led me to learn more about his sweeping movement in other U.S. industries in capturing management's interest in lasting improvement.

For years I've held that if you believe in your people enough, and if they feel good about what they do, great things can happen in your organization. I've known that respect for the individual and all people must come first in a win-win environment. Here was a philosophy that embraces that concept, a system that changes images and creates quality products. I became intrigued with how Dr. Deming's quality philosophy could transfer into a service organization—how it could apply to an educational intermediate unit such as the Riverside County Office of Education, whose "product" is service for our clients.

During the spring of 1992, I assigned staff to search out the best training on Dr. Deming's management philosophy. A seminar was selected which was being conducted personally by Dr. Deming in a neighboring county. Jerry Colapinto, the then new County Board of Education president—who is also part of the corporate world—and Dr. Aletrice Martin, of my leadership staff, went to his seminar, where they also met and talked with Dr. Ron Warwick. Both were highly enthusiastic about Dr. Deming's management philosophy and about how it could apply to our office to result in our doing business in a different way.

Ron Warwick was selected as our trainer. Our Board and leadership team have been through the first phase of the training. A pilot plan was developed to identify existing systems, which brought key people together in teams to receive the second and third phases of the Deming (Quality Education) seminars. A firm schedule is now in place for our employees to receive the balance of the training.

In the meantime, several teams are using what we've learned so far. An Accounts Payable work group reviewed their practice of examining each and every staff reimbursement claim for possible discrepancies—a very time-consuming practice. Using the Plan-Do-Study-Act Cycle, they learned that out of approximately 600 claims filed annually, only 10% were incorrect, and adjustments upward totaling $400 were being paid to employees over their original claims. In other words, the system was within statistical control, and these figures fell well within the upper and lower control limits described by Deming. A new random-sample review system for claims was instituted, and in less than a year we reduced by 90% the amount of time spent by Accounts Payable staff on this one task, with no significant discrepancies identified.

Another team, our Instructional Support Services Unit, looked at the process for approving and scheduling consultants. In the past, everyone booked their own consulting calendars according to their own understanding of the organization's priorities—there was no real system being uniformly used. In response, a system was designed so that every calendar decision is made by the team, consulting with each other to determine that consultant requests are matched to the organization's priorities. Decisions are now based on a clear aim for the end of the year. At the time of this writing, they are in the "Do" phase of Plan-Do-Study-Act. They have also designed an evaluation process which will be used to determine audience satisfaction.

Two significant things have evolved from our commitment to the Deming management philosophy:

1. **A plan to train all 23 school districts we serve so that the Deming system becomes a living process used throughout our county**

A "teaser" was offered to school-district leaders to test their interest. With the understanding that we will offer full training to school districts some time in the future, 15 of the 23 district superintendents, along with some key management people, attended the seminar. Community leaders such as the county PTA president, the chief probation officer, and a special education advocate also attended. Again, the training was received with a great deal of enthusiasm, and school districts are urging that their training begin soon.

2. **The formation of a Quality Systems Task Force to set the future direction of the County Office of Education**

A special opportunity to use the Deming process evolved in June 1994, when I was elected to another four-year term as County Superintendent. A 25-member Quality Systems Task Force was formed of employees from all levels of the organization, across divisions, including representatives from both the teachers and classified employees associations. This team is charged with studying the work of our office and developing a four-year plan. A vital source of information for the task force is the cumulative experiences and ideas of all employees. The final report is targeted for November 1994, and it will be shared with our school districts for their perceptions and input.

Priorities for our four-year agenda should be set by December 1994. The tools and process skills used to reach this goal are a direct result of our embracing the Deming philosophy. Planning teams will continue to be established and grouped to address our organizational priorities using the Plan-Do-Study-Act Cycle.

Although we've not yet completed the full training cycle, we are still able to take from what we've learned to mobilize our organization in the constant search for continuous improvement. Staff at the Riverside County Office of Education are already talking "systems"—they are looking at data to see how systems can be changed—they are beginning to think differently about how they do their jobs and how their jobs relate to other staff members.

As we continue to establish our process, it will be applied to the highest priorities of our organization.

> Dr. Dale S. Holmes, Ed.D.
> Riverside County Superintendent of Schools
> Riverside, CA

REPORT 4 FROM TALLAHASSEE, FLORIDA
"IMPLEMENTED FROM THE BOTTOM UP"

Florida, like many other states, is committed to educational reform. Although statewide reform has emerged as a theme repeatedly over the past 40 years, this initiative is novel in that it is fueled by economic realities, envisioned as long-term, and implemented from the bottom up.

Past reform efforts were viewed as politically expedient quick fixes initiated by state mandate with heavy penalties for noncompliance. Each served to add something to the system but never changed it. Systemic reform is the key to Florida's most recent initiative, an initiative driven by accountability at all levels. Such reform requires new skills, knowledge, and attitudes for all stakeholders. It also requires a clear local vision and new ways of work. This report briefly describes Florida's initiative, its incorporation of national efforts, and its focus on quality.

Recognizing that Florida students must possess new, higher-order skills to meet the demands of an emerging global economy, the changing landscape of the global economy, and the emerging educational requirements for student success, the Florida Legislature in early 1991 enacted a comprehensive educational reform and accountability law (Blueprint 2000). This law established a process to decentralize state and local school control, involve citizens in decision making, provide meaningful public reporting, and deliver high-level, relevant instruction for one central purpose: to improve all students' performance. The law also created a high-level commission co-chaired by the Lieutenant Governor and Commissioner of Education to conceptualize, direct, and evaluate the major policies, standards, and systems necessary for total reform.

The immediate output of this commission (the Florida Commission on Education Reform and Accountability) has been a series of foundation documents, standards, and policies. The Department of Education as an active partner has restructured itself and provided training for stakeholders, developed public school reports, promoted the establishment of local school advisory councils, assisted school-level annual plans, aligned a statewide initiative focusing on reform (Blueprint 2000), and spearheaded a massive public awareness campaign. Over the next three years, the department's priority will be curriculum, instruction, and assessment development issues.

These priorities are not intended to be developed, implemented, or evaluated in a top-down manner; rather, they will provide teachers and local curriculum designers with broad instructional frameworks, resource listings, training, and performance benchmarks.

The vision is that those closest to the students are best positioned to make decisions regarding the most appropriate means to facilitate a high-quality learning experience for all students. Our traditional model has provided structured, quality instruction more for the college-bound minority and less for the majority. The variable has been what is learned. Methodology and time have remained rigidly constant, true to the mass-production model of a hundred years ago. Students of yesteryear could be successful within this model.

However, today's students inherit the information age of global competition and exploding knowledge. All successful workers will need high-level academic and personal skills, which are contextual to work, community, and family. Many of these skills must be acquired at a high level regardless of the time necessary or the instructional means required by each student. These skills and competencies are well-profiled by the Secretary's Commission for Achieving Necessary Skills (SCANS). They include the abilities to perform such high-level tasks as acquiring and allocating resources, selecting appropriate technologies, evaluating and refining systems, acquiring and using information, etc. These are not typically the focus of our discipline-centered curriculum.

Therefore, when the Blueprint 2000 documents centered the SCANS competencies and skills as primary student-performance indicators, the realization that true systematic reform was intended became apparent to everyone involved. Parents, educators, and business people required a new vision of what schools could become. They needed to become informed and involved as allies of reform because of the comprehensive nature of the change. Massive public information campaign and reporting systems have been initiated at the local and state levels to create better community awareness and promote school involvement. School councils have been designated in law and empowered to develop school improvement plans.

These plans address the state's seven goals in whatever was deemed most appropriate for the improvement of that school's student performances. Because the assessment system for accountability is under development, much of the definition of student performance may be locally determined. Traditional indicators are used in the school's report card but may be supplemented by other local data. The plans are either accepted in their entirety by the district school boards or rejected for rework; they may only be amended by the school's councils.

Consensus is a powerful resource for systemic change. Systemic reform means everything potentially changes. As the individual subsystems merge and expand, the relationships between them also change and trigger another wave of subsystem change. The process is unending and defies accurate endpoint predictions. It does, however, lend itself to center on a clear vision, which each successive wave should more closely approximate. It should instill quality concepts as fundamental operating principles. Vision and quality are essential for what Peter Senge refers to as "learning organizations." Florida's Blueprint 2000 evokes notions of schools as learning organizations not only for students but also for teachers and administrators. Learning Organizations models require Florida's teachers not only to "teach" SCANS skills but to employ them at a high level each day as they work with students. The organizations require teachers to model quality instruction and integrate quality processes throughout instruction.

Of all the SCANS competencies most necessary to current teachers, the one centered on "systems" appears to have the most immediate potential, for several reasons:

1. Deming postulates that 85% of quality improvement comes from system improvement.

2. Teachers are generally neither taught about nor encouraged to investigate systems.

3. Public education represents a massive bureaucratic system whose structure begs efficiencies.

4. Data and feedback components related to learning and student success after school are becoming more sophisticated.

5. Ongoing reform efforts are disturbing various subsystems, prompting systematic examination.

Because the vision of Blueprint 2000 is drastically different from traditional practice in Florida's 2,700 schools, the Department of Education has initiated a number of collaborative pilot projects. These projects center on deep, systemic reform driven by student need, sound research, and Deming's principles. They incorporate learning organization concepts, involve business and postsecondary partners, and organize instruction around exit outcomes. These lighthouse-type projects produce possibilities for others to expand or adopt as each school learns its way to improvement. A brief description of two such projects follows to illustrate their contributions to reform:

In 1988-89, the department initiated the *Blueprint for Career Preparation*, which used broad goal statements for promoting articulated change in grades Pre-K through postsecondary. These changes were implemented within a single strand of pilot schools feeding students to each other (i.e., elementary, middle, high school, technical center, community college, and university). Over the years within these strands, curriculum changed, technology became more important, and student performance increased. One pilot is now either in a planning or operation phase within every district in Florida. This was a foundational program for the deeper reform represented by Blueprint 2000. More recently, teachers, administrators, and the public wanted models of what Blueprint 2000 might look like in practice.

During 1993-94, the state commissioned 15 career academies (Academies for Career Development and Applied Technology) to test the working assumptions, goals, and standards of Blueprint 2000. These academies are organized around an industry area (aerospace, health, etc.) as high school "schools-within-a-school," with a cadre of faculty that remain with an intact group of students for three to four years. The student population represented the same proportions of high-, medium-, and low-ability students as the school district population as a whole. Its demographic profile also mirrors the district's (race, socioeconomic status, gender, etc.).

These academies depend on postsecondary and business partners to define outcomes necessary for success. They hold learning outcomes constant for all students but vary time and instructional approach to accommodate individual students. Instructional technology, thematic units, and open facilities are readily observable. Preliminary student results indicate lower discipline rates, higher attendance rates, and improved test performance. Teachers appreciate the industry focus, collaboration with other adults, and the opportunity to be a "quality contributor" each day. They make decisions, initiate projects, link with employers, explore new technologies and knowledge bases, and learn with students.

The students, teachers, and administrators in these academies continue to learn about and use Deming's principles as ways of work because they are stepping into new territory. They need new skills that promote instructional flexibility and problem solving, generating continual improvement in student performance. Quality of learning, not quantity of teaching is the emerging paradigm. The academy staff generally embrace Deming's principles as guiding operational values. For example, principals and coordinators (management) are clearly responsible for the success of the broad curriculum models, community acceptance, appropriate facilities, and necessary district and state waivers (Points 2, 7, 9, 12, and 14 of Deming's 14 Points toward quality).

Academy teachers and administrators are learning new ways of work from specialized workshops, private sector training, and local seminars. Dr. Warwick's workshops have been sponsoring training for the academies since inception in 1993. A prominent electronics company that sponsors quality training for its team leaders and employees has extended that training to local academy teachers (as team leaders) and students (as employees). It is also engaged in ongoing quality support for the academy as if it were a unit of the company. A number of academies have joined local quality movements (councils) provided by business or education groups within their community. These networks are highly conducive to sustaining and supporting individual academies' efforts.

New solutions for persistent problems in education continue to be defined and implemented in microcosm. The vision of Blueprint 2000 and statewide reform will be realized only as we expand the knowledge and use of more effective systems within the context of quality.

Glenn Thomas
Bureau Chief: Florida Department of Education
Bureau of Career Development and
 Educational Improvement
Tallahassee, FL 32399
Phone: 904-488-0400

REPORT 5 FROM PERRIS, CALIFORNIA
"WORK BEGINS WITH SELF-ESTEEM"

The Perris Union High School District was plagued for a number of years with low self-esteem and poor quality of work in the area of maintenance and operations. Supervisors came and went. Even outside management consulting firms were discarded as losers. As the district searched for ways to improve, the Deming Philosophy of Management was discussed. The leads in each area of maintenance and operations met with the Assistant Superintendent of Business to discuss the possibility of implementing a shared decision-making model that has proved extremely successful. The following steps outline a brief history of how the process evolved. The Superintendent, Dr. Stephen C. Teele, and his cabinet, which included the Assistant Superintendent of Business, Dr. Donald Sauter, attended a workshop at the Riverside County Office of Education (RCOE) given by Dr. Ronald Warwick, an advocate of the Deming philosophy. Dr. Warwick had made a proposal to the County Superintendent, Dr. Dale Holmes, for a county-wide inoculation of processes included in the Deming philosophy of management.

The school district reviewed a contract from a neighboring school district where the transportation department had been "taken over" by the classified staff. We remodeled this contract, negotiated with the union, and set up a maintenance and operations board, including the four leads and the Assistant Superintendent of Business. For over a year now, the leads have continued to make positive reports to the school board, included other employees in the planning process and, in a word, "revolutionized" the maintenance and operations department. Self-esteem is of the highest order! Facilities are in better shape than ever.

Monies in the budget are saved, which, incidentally, are returned to purchase equipment and provide opportunities for training.

The success of this program is attested to by the administration, the employees and the Board of Trustees; but, above all, the results of cleaner, safer, better-maintained schools communicate a commitment to improvement and quality.

> Dr. Stephen C. Steele: Superintendent
> Perris Union High School District
> 1151 North A Street
> Perris, CA 92570-1090

DID YOU KNOW THAT WE PROVIDE PROFESSIONAL DEVELOPMENT?

The National Educational Service has a strong commitment to enhancing the lives of youth by producing top-quality, timely materials for the professionals who work with them. Our resource materials include books, videos, and professional development workshops in the following areas:

Creating the New American School

Gaining Parental Involvement and Community Support

School Based Management

Cooperative Learning

Reclaiming Youth at Risk

Multicultural Awareness

Discipline with Dignity

Our current mission focuses on celebrating diversity in the classroom and managing change in education.

NEED MORE COPIES OR ADDITIONAL RESOURCES ON THIS TOPIC?

Need more copies of this book? Want your own copy? Need additional resources on this topic? If so, you can order additional materials by using this form or by calling us at (800) 733-6786 or (812) 336-7700. Or you can order by FAX at (812) 336-7790.

Preview any resource for 30 days without obligation. If you are not completely satisfied, simply return it within 30 days of receiving it and owe nothing.

Title	Price	Quantity	Total
Beyond Piecemeal Improvements	$21.95		
Cooperative Classroom	$19.95		
Creating Learning Communities: The Role of the Teacher in the 21st Century	$18.95		
Creating the New American School	$19.95		
How Can We Create Thinkers? Questioning Strategies that Work	$22.95		
How Smart Schools Get and Keep Community Support	$19.95		
Leading Schools to Quality (video and leader's guide)	$250.00		
Parents Assuring Student Success	$21.95		
Principal As Staff Developer	$16.95		
School Based Management	$21.95		
Sharing Thinking Strategies	$22.95		
Teaching Students to Think	$21.95		
Shipping & Handling: Please add 7% of order total, or a minimum of $3.00, if check or credit card information is not enclosed.			

TOTAL _____

❏ Check enclosed with order ❏ Please bill me (P.O. #_____)
❏ VISA or MasterCard ❏ Money Order

Credit Card No._____ Exp. Date _____
Cardholder Signature _____

SHIP TO:
Name_____ Title _____
Organization _____
Address _____
City_____ State_____ ZIP _____
Phone_____ FAX _____

MAIL TO:
National Educational Service
1252 Loesch Road
P.O. Box 8
Bloomington, IN 47402